Psychology

Cognitive Development

BROWN
BEAR
BOOKS

Published by Brown Bear Books Limited

4877 N. Circulo Bujia
Tucson
AZ 85718
USA

First Floor
9–17 St. Albans Place
London N1 0NX
UK

www.brownreference.com

© 2010 The Brown Reference Group Ltd

ISBN: 978-1-936333-17-2

Editorial Director: Lindsey Lowe
Managing Editor: Tim Cooke
Project Director: Laura Durman
Editor: Helen Dwyer
Designer: Barry Dwyer
Picture Researcher: Barry Dwyer

Library of Congress Cataloging-in-Publication Data available upon request

Contents

Introduction

Psychology **forms part of the Curriculum Connections series. Each of the six volumes of the set covers a particular aspect of psychology: History of Psychology; The Brain; Cognitive Development; Intellectual Development; The Individual and Society; and Abnormal Psychology.**

About this set

Each volume in *Psychology* features illustrated chapters, providing in-depth information about each subject. The chapters are all listed in the contents pages of each book. Each volume can be studied to provide a comprehensive understanding of the different aspects of psychology. However, each chapter may also be studied independently.

Within each chapter there are two key aids to learning that are to be found in color sidebars located in the margins of each page:

Curriculum Context sidebars indicate to the reader that a subject has a particular relevance to certain key state and national psychology guidelines and curricula. They highlight essential information or suggest useful ways for students to consider a subject or to include it in their studies.

Glossary sidebars define key words within the text.

At the end of the book, a summary **Glossary** lists the key terms defined in the volume. There is also a list of further print and Web-based resources and a full volume index.

Fully captioned illustrations play an important role throughout the set, including photographs and explanatory diagrams.

About this book

Cognitive Development analyzes the nature of developmental change throughout childhood. We begin to acquire our cognitive abilities before birth with the growth of the fetus. Research shows that, as the fetal brain develops, so too do the fetus's cognitive and perceptual skills.

From the moment of birth infants seem able to recognize external stimuli and even to discriminate between them. This volume identifies the important stages that contribute to infant development and also examines the ingenious methods devised by scientists to measure cognitive abilities in people so young.

This book also analyzes two of the most important theories of cognitive development, proposed by Lev Vygotsky and Jean Piaget. While Vygostky saw children as "apprentices" who learn from more experienced individuals, Piaget regarded children as "inquiring scientists" who learn by experimenting with their environment.

The volume explores the complex study of perceptual development: how infants form ideas about how the world works from the sensory information that they receive. Memory development is another fascinating area of developmental psychology which is analyzed in this book. The emotional development of infants is also explored, along with their ability to learn complex social and problem solving skills.

Fetal Development

We imagine that life for a fetus must be dark and quiet, with little change in the environment. Recent research, however, has suggested that the womb has a vast array of stimulating experiences with which to shape the fetal brain.

Human beings are created when a reproductive cell from a man, a sperm, comes together with a reproductive cell from a woman, an egg.

Central nervous system

Approximately three weeks after fertilization, one-third of the fertilized egg (known as the ectoderm) begins developing into the central nervous system (CNS). This section of the ectoderm begins to fold inward and forms a hollow cylinder called the neural tube, which will develop the spinal cord at the rear end and the forebrain and midbrain at the front end. The spinal cord end divides into a series of segments, while the front end forms a series of bulges. By five weeks these bulges have formed into the beginnings of the brain. Along its circumference, the neural tube develops into the sensory and motor systems.

Nerve cells

The developed human nervous system is primarily made up of two types of cells—neurons and glial cells. Neurons are nerve cells that communicate with each other, either individually or in collections of millions or billions. Glial cells supply energy to neurons.

In the developing brain, new cells are built in proliferative zones located in fluid-filled chambers called ventricles. Here cells are given their speciality. By 18 weeks most cells have migrated to the brain area, where they will stay for the rest of the person's life. Once a neuron has settled into its permanent site, it begins to grow tentaclelike extensions from its main

Central nervous system

The brain and the spinal cord.

Curriculum Context

Students should be able to identify the component parts of the central nervous system.

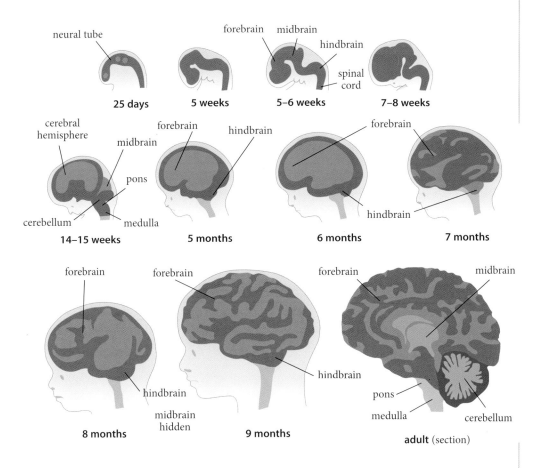

neural tube | forebrain midbrain | hindbrain | spinal cord

25 days | **5 weeks** | **5–6 weeks** | **7–8 weeks**

cerebral hemisphere | forebrain | hindbrain | forebrain
midbrain | pons
cerebellum | medulla | hindbrain

14–15 weeks | **5 months** | **6 months** | **7 months**

forebrain | forebrain | forebrain | midbrain
hindbrain
hindbrain | midbrain hidden | pons | medulla | cerebellum

8 months | **9 months** | **adult** (section)

cell body toward other neurons. These extensions are called axons and dendrites. Each neuron grows one axon. Axons transmit signals. They stretch out to make connections with neighboring neurons or neurons that are farther removed. Dendrites are short and branching; they grow from along the cell body of a neuron and receive signals from other neurons.

Synaptogenesis

The growth of dendrites is called synaptogenesis. Synapses are the connections that dendrites and axons make with each other for neurons to communicate with one another. The messenger that carries these messages is a neurotransmitter, a small amount of chemical that is released from one neural element to another across a synapse. One neuron may have tens of thousands of synapses.

The very first stages of our brains appear at about 25 days after conception, with the emergence of the neural tube. At about five weeks the brain stem appears, which will develop into the medulla, pons, and the forebrain. The midbrain is not visible as a separate structure after five months. The major structures of the medulla will form between the seventh and eighth weeks, and the pons appears after the eighth week. The cortex is the last part to develop.

The fetal brain makes far more connections than it will eventually need. In later life, synapses are pruned. The critical factor that determines that a synapse should be pruned is whether or not it is used. Synapses are based on the experiences of the individual, so experience literally shapes the brain. Electrical activity stabilizes the synapse and fixes it in place.

Making Connections

One question that still puzzles researchers is how a neuron knows to which other neurons it should send its connections. Neuroscientists have discovered that experiences actually shape the way the human brain forms. When a neuron has migrated to the area of the brain to which it has been genetically programmed to migrate, it sends out a thin offshoot—a growth cone—to "sniff out" the right cells that it should "speak with."

The growth cone sends offshoots in all directions, each trying to detect target neurons. To reach their targets, these offshoots move toward other neurons that emit specific chemical signatures and rely on magnetic fields caused by electrical activity. On contact the dendrite forms a synapse, and the cells begin to communicate with each other. With use over time, these connections become reinforced.

The creation and pruning of synapses explains two critical factors in human development. First, that the powerful human brain is capable of almost anything. If you speak in many languages to a baby, it will learn all the languages that you speak. That is because it still has many synaptic connections related to language. Second, that adults find it harder to learn new cognitive tasks as they get older, since unused synapses may have been pruned.

Cognitive

Relating to the gaining of knowledge and understanding through thought, experience, and the senses.

From eight to twelve weeks right up until birth, the only development will be in existing parts and their functions. Independent neuromotor activity begins, and the fetus now has control of its movement: The head and abdomen make slight movements.

The cerebral cortex

The part of our brain that gives us the unique behavior of humans is known as the cerebral cortex. In the adult it appears as the wrinkly surface of the brain. The wrinkles are known as sulci and they appear to arrive in three stages. The primary sulci, which are common in all humans, begin to be defined at approximately 20 weeks. Tertiary sulci are specific to the individual person and finish fully developing a year after birth.

Myelination

In adults, axons are covered in a fatty substance, myelin, that insulates them. The process of myelin growth is known as myelination. It starts in the spinal cord at five months but does not take place in the brain until after the seventh month, continuing up until birth. Myelination continues through infancy. It is so important that certain cognitive functions will not fully develop until myelination has occurred in parts of the brain related to those cognitive functions.

Environmental Factors

In the first three months an adverse environment can have the most devastating effects on the developing fetus. Teratogens include the age of the mother and the father, the mother's diet, the mother's health, whether or not the mother is stressed physically or psychologically, and chemicals in the mother's bloodstream, such as nicotine or alcohol.

If a pregnant woman is under stress, her emotional state can lead to complications in pregnancy and labor. Some studies have linked high stress levels to premature babies, low birthweights in newborn babies, and later behavioral difficulties. Stress in the mother may divert blood flow to her major organs rather than sending the blood to the fetus, causing a temporary oxygen deficiency in the fetus.

Cerebral cortex
The outer layer of the brain that plays an important part in consciousness.

Cognitive functions
Those behaviors that are driven from the cortex of the brain and are also high-level processing, such as memory recall, language, or reasoning.

Teratogens
Environmental factors that can affect the development of the fetus.

Alcohol

Alcohol is a teratogen. In the maternal bloodstream it passes to the fetus and anesthetizes the fetus's frontal lobes. As the pregnant mother drinks more alcohol, the anesthetized area progresses from the frontal lobes to the midbrain areas, such as the thalamus, effectively rendering the fetus unconscious. If the amount of alcohol continues to rise in the fetal bloodstream, then the brain stem will become anesthetized, which will stop the flow of blood to the fetal brain and kill the fetus. Alcohol can also cause a condition known as Fetal Alcohol Syndrome (FAS). A newborn baby with FAS has a lower birthweight than other newborn babies and later in life may have cognitive deficits. People with FAS have eyes set farther apart and a slightly larger forehead than is normal, and they often have abnormalities of internal organs.

Nicotine is a teratogen—something outside the fetus that will affect its development. Even if a pregnant woman does not smoke, if someone smokes near her, the fetus will be "smoking" too.

Temporal cortex

Part of the cerebral cortex; it plays an important part in hearing, speech, vision, and long-term memory.

Smoking

If a mother smokes while she is pregnant, she dramatically increases the chance of miscarrying her baby or prematurely giving birth. Premature birth and a low birthweight increase the chance of cognitive deficits and neurological damage for the baby.

Nicotine disrupts the flow of oxygen-filled blood to the fetus by restricting the flow or increasing the flow in bursts. Some scientists suggest that this causes alterations in the fetal "breathing" pattern, which continue after birth. When scientists introduced nicotine into rat fetuses, it seemed to slow down the growth of neurons in areas of the temporal cortex.

Fetal behavior and cognition

There are specific times in development before which certain learning must take place. These windows in time are called critical periods and they occur during the pruning of synaptic connections, when neural pathways are refined. There are critical periods for many cognitive skills. Neurons are pruned even while the fetus learns in the womb. Critical periods for learning how to use some senses, such as taste and smell, occur at this point.

Touch

The somatosensory system, which is responsible for tactile sensations, or touch, is not fully developed at birth, but is nevertheless in an advanced state. That is why newborn babies are particularly happy when they are held and caressed. By five weeks an embryo is responsive to other somatosensory influences, such as stimulation near the mouth and nose. The basis for the sensation of pain seems to emerge before the end of the 14th week.

Embryo
An unborn human baby in the eight weeks after conception. After eight weeks it is called a fetus.

Learning in the womb

A fetus can learn while it is in the womb. One type of learning is habituation. It occurs when a stimulus is presented repeatedly, during which time it becomes less interesting. When a new stimulus is presented, the interest of the fetus increases.

Classical conditioning is a more advanced form of learning, and studies show that a fetus also learns this way. It is demonstrated when two stimuli are paired together and an association is formed between them. Ultrasound studies have shown that mothers who listen to particular music and relax when listening to it condition the fetus to relax to the music as well.

Ultrasound
Sound waves with a frequency above human hearing that are often used in medical imaging.

The vestibular system

Motion and balance are some of the most developed senses with which babies are born. That is because they have felt the movements of their mothers and their own movements for many months in the womb. Our sense of movement and balance is perceived by

The Fetus and Language

Human brains are designed to learn language. During the first sixth months in the womb, the planum temporale, the area of the brain related to language production and understanding, begins to grow larger on the left side of the brain compared to the right. Research with premature babies has shown that by the end of the sixth month, a fetus has a specialized left hemisphere language area: It can hear words better in the right ear, which means that information is traveling to the left hemisphere (the brain swaps information coming from one side of the body to the opposite side of the brain.)

Two further factors indicate that the human brain is wired to learn aspects of language before birth. First, adults can detect phonemes (the smallest boundaries or units of sound in a language) only in languages with which they are familiar. Fetuses and newborn babies, however, can detect these boundaries even in unfamiliar languages, which allows them to concentrate on learning more complex rules of language. Research has shown that newborn babies increase their sucking rate on a dummy when they detect new phonemes, suggesting that they recognize them as new. Second, there is evidence that by the end of the fifth month, a fetus is able to detect the difference between similar-sounding phonemes, indicating that this ability is present in the forming brain.

Vestibular system

A series of liquid-filled canals located in the inner ear.

the vestibular system. At five months the vestibular system is completely formed and functioning.

As the fetus grows, it runs out of space to move in. From the sixth month of pregnancy, kicking appears to decrease, and full body movements, such as squirming, increase because of the growing lack of space.

Development of visual abilities

Vision begins when the eye starts to form in the four-week-old embryo. At eight weeks the optic nerve has formed. It is a pathway for visual information that will pass to the visual areas located at the back of the brain in an area known as the occipital cortex. It is here that the most complex aspects of visual cognition, such as movement detection, fully develop after birth.

Two independent pathways in the brain, called streams, complement each other. The "what" stream

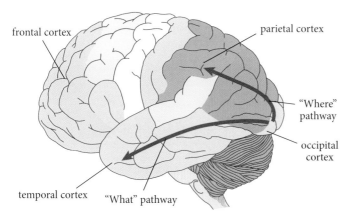

frontal cortex

parietal cortex

"Where" pathway

occipital cortex

temporal cortex

"What" pathway

The "what" and "where" pathways in the brain help us understand what we see. The "what" pathway, which travels from the occipital to the temporal cortex, helps us identify what we see. The "where" pathway, which goes from the occipital to the parietal cortex, helps us locate what we see relative to ourselves.

travels from the occipital cortex to the temporal cortex. It is responsible for our understanding of what an object is and does. The "where" stream proceeds from the occipital cortex to the parietal cortex. This pathway is vital for an understanding of spatial relations.

Maximum density of synapses in the "where" stream occurs at four months after birth, while the "what" stream requires another eight months of synaptic growth. This explains why newborn babies are better at tracking an object, than recognizing the difference between two similar objects.

Taste

Taste is one of the most developed senses at birth. A collection of cells in the fetus's mouth, the taste buds, detect chemicals in the amniotic sac. These cells are tuned to detect specific tastes: sweet, sour, salty, or bitter. The first taste buds develop at eight weeks. At around the 14th week, nerves from the taste buds are connected to the developing cortex in the brain. From then on the fetus will be able to taste the amniotic fluid surrounding it. The taste buds send information to the medulla, which is located in the brain stem. The brain stem is also important for swallowing and salivation, and the sensation of taste triggers these behaviors. From the medulla, the taste input moves to the cortical areas of the brain. That is where tastes

Occipital cortex
Part of the cerebral cortex concerned with visual processing.

Parietal cortex
Part of the cerebral cortex concerned with integrating sensory information.

Amniotic sac
The fluid-filled membrane that encloses the fetus.

are registered, and the drinking baby is made aware of the taste of the amniotic fluid.

Smell
The sensory system that is related to smell is known as the olfactory system. It begins to function at between six and seven months. Odor molecules bind to the nasal mucus, sending information about the odor to a part of the brain called the olfactory bulb, which processes the smell and sends the information to a structure in the brain known as the thalamus. From there the information moves to many different areas, but it must reach the primary olfactory cortex on the surface of the brain before the fetus becomes aware of the smell. From the sixth month the fetus smells the food the mother eats, as well as tastes it.

Hearing
During the fourth month of pregnancy a fetus will begin to hear sounds from outside the uterus. Sound waves set up vibrations that travel through the amniotic fluid surrounding the fetus. These vibrations are detected by the fetal ear and channeled to the eardrum. In the ear three tiny bones, known as the hammer, anvil, and stirrup, vibrate together. This vibration amplifies the sound and transmits it to the inner ear, which is filled with a gooey fluid. In the fluid, tiny hairs detect the vibration and turn it into electrical impulses, which are sent through the auditory nerve into the brain to the primary auditory cortex. From four months of age the fetus can hear everything that the mother can hear, although the range is limited. Throughout the remainder of the pregnancy (and after birth) the detection of the range of sound and the volume will increase.

Motor development
The motor system matures slowly because motor activity is exceptionally complex. Unlike sensory

Can a Fetus Remember?

One thing that everyone knows about very early childhood is that it is eventually forgotten: You cannot recall how it felt to have your diaper changed. This phenomenon is known as infantile amnesia. It came as a great surprise to many researchers to discover that the fetus has a fully functioning memory. There are two lines of evidence for this finding: research with fetuses and research with newborn babies.

A simple form of learning is sensory-motor learning. Simple forms of life, such as worms and microscopic organisms, use this form of learning to remember how to act when their environment changes in a specific way. This can also be seen in a fetus: If the mother's abdomen is rubbed on one side, the fetus will move to the other side because it has learned that this is a way of avoiding unwanted stimulation.

Studies with newborn babies clearly show that they remember experiences in the womb. Music that a baby frequently heard before being born will often stop him from crying when it is played. This is not the case with music the baby hears for the first time outside the womb.

systems, in which information about the world is taken from the world and sent to the brain, information in the motor system travels in two directions during the most simple of motions.

The primary motor cortex (PMC) is a strip of tissue that contains a map of the human body. The map gives more space to parts of the body with groups of muscles that use specialized movements, such as the face and lips, compared to muscle groups that perform simple movements, such as the torso. The PMC develops around the eighth week of fetal development, but it requires many years of "training" to define the specific areas of the body that are mapped within it. Voluntary movements are initiated in specific areas of the PMC, each related to different parts of the body. Electrical impulses travel down a special pathway, called the corticospinal tract, to the spinal cord. Electrical activity is discharged into the muscle of the desired site of action, and the muscle is "excited" into making a movement.

Torso
The trunk of the human body.

Infant Cognition

Adults take many of their thinking processes for granted, but most of the things that seem second nature to them had to be learned. How do babies work out effective methods of recognizing external stimuli? How do they learn to talk and walk?

People are equipped from birth with a general mechanism that helps them pick up and retain information. One important part of this mechanism is the ability to imitate. Even very young babies can imitate some facial expressions and may be able to reproduce fairly complex emotional expressions such as happiness and sadness. Two-day-old infants will copy the head movements of adults. By the time babies are two weeks old, if an adult sticks out a tongue, they will stick out theirs. Only about a month later, babies can mimic movements some time after they saw the original action. This is known as deferred imitation. In order to demonstrate deferred imitation, a baby must have some kind of mental representation.

Mental representation

An image or idea that is stored in the memory and can be accessed at will.

Responding to stimuli

Neonates (newborn babies) can control their eye movements from birth, and researchers use this behavior to test what babies know. Newborns will follow with their eyes a simplified pattern if it is moved slowly sideways away from the midline of their vision. This response is known as tracking. Researchers can

Infants learn facial expressions such as smiling by copying the adults around them, and there is some evidence that they can remember and repeat these expressions spontaneously from about six weeks of age.

record changes in the baby's visual sensitivity by examining differences in his tracking responses.

Babies' understanding of what they are looking at is determined through habituation studies in which they are repeatedly shown the same stimulus. At first they show interest and fixate on the object; but as they become familiar with the stimulus, they are less responsive to it. Eventually they are said to be "habituated." Then they are given a new stimulus, and their responses to both stimuli are measured.

Curriculum Context

Habituation is one of several research methods used with young children that students may be asked to explain.

The technique most often used to test what babies know is the forced-choice preferential looking procedure. The experimenter will show the baby several similar stimuli for a fixed period until the baby becomes familiar with them. Then the experimenter will show the baby two fresh stimuli: one a new stimulus from the familiarized category and another from a new category. The researcher then records which stimulus the baby looks at for longer. If the baby shows a preference for the new category, it implies that the baby has formed a representation of the familiar stimulus and no longer needs to look at it.

Concepts

A concept may be defined as a way we group different objects into categories in order to think about them and to recognize them when we see them again. It may be a concrete image or an abstract one. We can form concepts of groups of events, objects, and situations that we regard as related. Our concepts divide the world into classes. In order to have the concept "ovens can burn," we must have two mental pictures: one of ovens, the other of what a burn is like.

Concrete
Existing in a physical form.

Abstract
Existing as an idea but having no physical existence.

People must divide their knowledge of the objects and information in the world into a manageable number of categories. This has the advantage of reducing the amount of information to remember. It also enables people to recognize new stimuli as members of an already familiar category.

Development of concepts

People seem to put many categories of objects into hierarchies. In 1975 Eleanor Rosch conducted studies of how these hierarchies are structured. She found that they tend to build up from a single instance, such as "my dog," to increasingly abstract concepts, such as "dogs." We can retain a mental image of how dogs look even though it is highly generalized. But we can have no generic image that covers every mammal species because the category is too large and diverse to be retained in the mind as a single entity. Thus the basic level of recognition is based on how alike members of a category look. This is known as perceptual similarity. By the time babies are three to four months old they are able to categorize objects at the basic level.

Recognizing Cats and Dogs

How do infants form concepts, and can this be measured? In 1997 Janine Spencer studied the abilities of four-month-old infants. The stimuli were 36 color pictures of cats and dogs. These pictures were placed to the far left and right of the children's field of vision, and their responses were measured by noting whether their eyes moved from one stimulus to the other.

First, the babies were shown six pairs of either cats or dogs to familiarize them with one type of animal. They were then shown a pair of hybrid animals in the preference test trials. The stimuli for the preference test included six sets of hybrid cat-and-dog pictures made up of various cats and

dogs that were different from those the babies had seen in the familiarization part of the test— some had the head of a cat on the body of a dog, others the head of a dog on the body of a cat.

When researchers compared the lengths of time the infants looked at the different hybrid (those with mismatching heads and bodies) stimuli, they found that the infants spent longer on those with a new head than on those with a familiar head and a new body. These preference results suggest that information from the head and face region rather than the rest of the body is essential for infants to distinguish between animal species such as these.

In the early 1990s Jean Mandler argued that perceptual and conceptual categorization are basically independent. She began by suggesting that if the way things look is the basis for developing conceptual categories, then infants should be able to distinguish between objects that are visually different. Yet her experiments showed that, although nine-month-olds could make categorical distinctions between some broad categories (for example, tell the difference between birds and airplanes), they could not necessarily distinguish between some basic-level categories, such as dogs and rabbits.

In 1996 Paul Quinn and Peter Eimas suggested that babies form categories through the use of both visual and conceptual information. Early in life, babies receive most of their information about the world through what they see and thus form most of their categorical groupings on the basis of visual similarity. As children develop, they learn more about objects in the world, and their ability to make categories becomes increasingly conceptual in nature.

This child has seen something interesting. Infants develop concepts and can categorize objects at about 3 or 4 months. At 12 months this child will only be able to say a few words, but over the next few years he will develop an extensive vocabulary.

Language

Learning to speak plays an important part in the development of children's abilities to form concepts and identify categories of objects. As soon as children develop verbal skills, they are able to use language to define and categorize what they see.

We acquire language at birth if not before. Within a few days of birth, babies can distinguish between the languages they heard while they were in the womb and other languages. Between the ages of seven and ten months, babies begin to babble, making noises such as "ba ba ba" or "da da da." These are phonemes, the smallest units of speech.

Up to the age of about 12 months, infants babble using all possible phoneme sounds. By the time children near their first birthdays, they will normally have learned to say a few words. The number of words they will learn grows rapidly in the first few years of life. When they are six years old, children have learned between 6,000 and 9,000 words.

Knowing how to say a few words is not the same as being able to communicate using language. Language involves understanding what the words mean individually and in relation to other words.

Constraints

In 1988 Ellen Markman and Gwyn Wachtel proposed that there are innate or inborn constraints on learning word meanings, and that babies are born with an instinct to make certain assumptions when they hear new words. When infants hear a new word to refer to an object, they assume it refers to the whole object. They do not consider the possibility that it may refer to a part or parts of the object or to what it is made of.

Another constraint is taxonomic. For example, children may assume that "cat" and "dog" are from the same category because they are both animals, but have greater difficulty in making the link between "door" and "key," which, though often related, have no obvious visual similarity to link them. Infants assume that labels refer to objects within the same category.

Another constraint is mutual exclusivity, which prevents infants from giving more than one label to any object. Pairs of words such as "dog" and "pet" cannot coexist in their minds. This gives no clue as to

Constraints
Limitations or restrictions.

Taxonomic
Concerned with classification.

how, by the age of about four, children have learned to make distinctions between words that refer to parts of objects, such as "tail," and those that refer to the objects themselves, such as "dog." Research by Markman and Wachtel into how children learn new words suggests that they assume that any new word describing an object refers to the whole object. They do not recognize two words used to describe the same object. When they hear a new word to describe an object with which they are already familiar, they think the new word refers to a part of the object.

Curriculum Context

Students may find it useful to examine the role played by constraints in language development in young children.

Some psychologists think that children do not have innate constraints at all. Rather, they have only biases to favor some assumptions over others. According to this argument, if circumstances alter, children will adapt and learn new words in a different way.

Age and Language Learning

Children around the world learn language at approximately the same age. In order to test whether or not there is a sensitive period for learning language, researchers began to study the language skills of children who had been abused and had experienced little human contact. Take the case of Genie, a little girl from Los Angeles, California. At the age of 20 months Genie was locked in a room in her parents' house until she was nearly 14 years old. No one was allowed to talk to her. If she made any noise at all, her parents would beat her. Genie's environment was emotionally as well as linguistically deprived.

Once Genie was found, over a period of years she was taught to speak. Her comprehension and vocabulary developed well, but her grasp of grammar never developed to the same extent as that of normal children. Other similar cases also support the idea that there is a critical period for learning the structure of language.

Innate or learned?
Some early researchers believed that language was acquired incidentally through general learning processes; others maintained that it came about as a result of innate predispositions. Learning a language involves making new connections between nerve cells.

If we were born with all the connections fully formed, we might not be able to learn anything new.

Learned argument

In the 1950s a debate raged between two schools of thought about language development. One group of theories was headed by B. F. Skinner and the other by Noam Chomsky. For Skinner every focus of psychology can be explained by observable behavior alone. According to Skinner, exposure to the environment provides the conditions for learning. We are born with an innate ability to learn, but everything we learn depends on the environment in which we live.

Skinner attempted to give a working explanation of how children learn language. Specifically, he was interested in the variables that control what he termed language behavior. He argued that the determining variables could be described entirely in terms of "stimulus, reinforcement, and deprivation."

According to behaviorist theory, we learn language through what Skinner called "operant conditioning." At first, babies utter sounds at random. People around them reinforce the sounds that resemble adult speech by displaying approval—smiling, paying attention—and by talking to them. Thus encouraged, the babies repeat these reinforced sounds. Infants also imitate the sounds they hear adults making, and the adults encourage them to make them again. As reinforcement continues, infants learn to produce meaningful speech by generalizing from their experience.

In contrast to Skinner, Noam Chomsky argued that, although reinforcement and imitation contribute to language development, they do not fully explain it. The rules of language and the fine distinctions in the meaning of words are so numerous and complex that

Curriculum Context

Some curricula may ask students to compare the views of Chomsky and Skinner.

Variable

Something whose value is subject to change.

Behaviorist

Relating to the theory that behavior can be explained by conditioning alone.

they could not all be acquired simply by reinforcement and imitation.

Language acquisition device

Young children around the world seem to learn language at about the same age. They do so without receiving enough feedback to teach them the rules of language. Chomsky suggested that children must be born with an innate mechanism in the brain, which he termed the language acquisition device (LAD). The LAD is triggered when children have learned enough words to form sentences and understand what they mean. That helps them acquire a fully functioning language. It does not matter which language children hear, the LAD has a universal grammar.

This baby from Botswana will have no more difficulty learning her native language than children born in any other parts of the world will have learning their native languages. Young children also seem to learn language at about the same age.

Pidgin and Creole

Derek Bickerton showed that part of the evidence for an innate predisposition to particular grammars is the way children convert pidgins into creoles. Pidgin is a simplified language with very little grammatical structure, and its word order is changeable and haphazard. There are none of the compensating inflections found in many languages. (Inflections are alterations to words to indicate tense, number, gender, or other grammatical differences.) Creole is any language made up of elements of two or more other languages.

In a single generation, though not necessarily the first, children brought up hearing only a pidgin language develop a complete new creole language with its own new rules of grammar. The grammars of creoles all around the world are remarkably similar even though they arise independently. Such processes strongly suggest that children do not learn language only as a result of imitation and reinforcement.

Pidgins and Creoles for the Deaf

Before 1979 deaf children in Nicaragua were not taught sign language; instead, they were forced to lip read. In the playground these children came up with a makeshift sign system they used at home. Now known as LSN (*Lenguaje de Señas Nicaragüense*, Spanish for Nicaraguan Sign Language), it does not have a consistent grammar: it is a pidgin sign language. Children who were four years or younger when they joined the school were exposed to the already existing LSN. As they grew up, their mature sign system turned out to be quite different from LSN. It had a consistent grammar. Like a real language, this new creole sign language allowed children to be far more expressive in their conversations. This language is now recognized as distinct from LSN and is referred to as ISN. Basically, ISN is a creole that the deaf Nicaraguan children spontaneously created from their knowledge of pidgin LSN.

The Modular Mind

In 1985 Jerry Fodor claimed that the mind is made up of two different types of system for thinking: input systems and central systems. The job of an input system is to understand sensory input, such as the information that reaches our brains through our eyes or ears. Once the input system has made sense of the incoming information, it can be passed on to the central thinking systems.

Modular
Self-contained and separate from each other.

Fodor suggested that all these input systems are modular. What goes on inside a module, such as the seeing module, is not available to other parts of the brain until the module has finished processing it. He argued that we are born with the structure already in place for the development of these mechanisms. In contrast to input systems, Fodor argued, central systems are slow, higher-level processes that have access to information from anywhere within the cognitive system. Babies are born with these innate modules in place.

Annette Karmiloff-Smith explained children's cognitive development with a modified version of Fodor's theory.

A young girl plays with building blocks. At the age of about four children can balance blocks of both even and uneven weight. A few years later they appear to have taken a reverse step and are able to balance only even-weight blocks. In the final stage they can balance blocks of even and uneven weight again, as their thought processes have developed to a level where they can solve the problem.

She made a distinction between innate modules, which have specific functions, and modularization, that is, the process by which the brain becomes specialized only as a result of developmental changes. So, babies are born with some innate predispositions, but without specific environmental input these predispositions will never be realized. The environment does not simply trigger the development of these innate predispositions; it actually affects the resulting structure of the brain.

Karmiloff-Smith also argued that in order to increase our knowledge, our minds can use any information we have already stored in our memory (innate or not) to modify our mental representations. This re-formed knowledge, in turn, results in the development of new modules that are specialized for receiving different kinds of sensory information.

The development of different types of knowledge, however, does not progress equally, according to Karmiloff-Smith. It depends on the individual; for example, some children's knowledge of math develops more slowly than their understanding of grammatical rules.

Curriculum Context

Students should be aware of differing views about the steps involved in processing information.

Perceptual Development

Perception is the bridge between the mind and the external world. By perceiving sensory information, we form beliefs and ideas about how the world works. Perceiving the world is possible only through a large number of complex biological processes.

Psychologists distinguish between sensation and perception. Sensation is the measuring ability of our senses to pick up information about the body. The data thus gathered are sent to the brain, where they are interpreted—that is perception. Perception is a learned process, at least to some substantial extent. Through experience the developing child learns to distinguish between the information from its different senses.

Psychologists are eager to measure the growth of perception in infants, but infants are not easy to test. They cannot talk, they are unable to follow verbal instructions, and they cannot point out objects. Consequently, researchers have had to devise a range of novel and ingenious measures to study how children's perceptual abilities develop.

Curriculum Context

Students should be able to explain the difficulties that occur in measuring the growth of perception in infants.

Many of the techniques used to test the development of infants' visual perception rely on watching their eye movements. The most common methods of studying infant vision rely on the techniques of preferential looking and habituation.

Preferential looking

In the classic preferential looking test, two stimuli are presented to a child at the same time. The objects are placed in front of the infant at eye level, one to the left of the nose, the other to the right. Researchers then measure how long the child looks at each stimulus. If the child looks at both stimuli for the same length of time, that is probably because the infant cannot tell them apart. However, if the child looks at one stimulus for longer than the other, then he or she is probably differentiating between the two stimuli.

Infants will fixate on objects and people until they become familiar with them. They then lose interest and look away. This process is termed habituation. Studies of habituation have provided a wealth of information about the development of perceptual processes. For example, infants will be shown a stimulus for a set period over and over again. Once they have become "habituated," they are shown a new stimulus. If the infants' interests revive in response to the new stimulus, this indicates that the infants can discriminate between the two stimuli.

Holding a brightly colored toy in front of a crying baby is often a successful way of stopping her from crying, but then she will lose interest in the toy and start crying again. This process, called habituation, has been studied to reveal how perceptual processes develop in young children.

Visual evoked potentials

Preferential looking and habituation techniques observe the overt behavior of children. By contrast, physiological measures such as visual evoked potentials (VEPs) measure electrical activity in infants' brains. Whenever nerve cells are active, they produce small electrical currents known as potentials. The electrical activity can be measured by placing electrodes on an infant's head over the area of the brain that is responsible for vision. As the infant looks at the stimuli, changes in electrical activity are recorded on a computer.

Contrast sensitivity

The other main way of assessing early visual acuity is by testing infants' contrast sensitivity, or their ability to differentiate an object from its background. Contrast sensitivity is normally measured by getting people to look at spatial gratings. These are grids that have

Electrode
The conductor through which electricity enters or leaves an object.

Visual acuity
Sharpness or keenness of sight.

parallel bars with a series of gaps between them. They test the ability to discern what is behind the bars. The distance between the bars and the brightness (luminance) of both the grating itself and the object behind it can be varied in the test in order to establish the limits of people's sensitivity.

Depth perception

By about eight to nine months of age, infants begin to crawl, and for the first time they are able to explore their environment on their own. They are able to move themselves around objects such as furniture and can reach out and grab things. That suggests that they can perceive depth and the distance between objects. To be able to see the world in depth has numerous advantages. Luckily, there are a number of visual clues that help us see the world in three dimensions.

One of the most important aids to seeing in depth is stereoscopic vision. Depth perception based on stereoscopic vision depends on having a slightly different image received by each eye, and having two eyes that point in the same direction. When we look at something that is near us, we can see it with both eyes. This is known as crossed disparity. Hold up your finger directly in front of your nose, and look at it. Your eyes will move together so they can both see it. However, when you look at faraway objects, your eyes diverge, so you see a different image in each eye. This is known as uncrossed disparity.

In the visual cortex there are cells that respond to crossed disparity. There are also cells that respond to uncrossed disparity and sense objects that are far away. Look at an object in the distance. Now close your left eye and look at it. If you now close your right eye, and look at the same object with your left eye, it will appear to have moved. This ability to see two different images allows us to see in depth. It is known as stereopsis.

Curriculum Context

Students may find it useful to list the ways in which an infant begins to understand that we exist in a three-dimensional world.

Visual cortex

The area of the brain concerned with vision.

Human infants start to show sensitivity to stereopsis from as early as 11 to 13 weeks. However, stereopsis is not the only function that enables us to see depth. If we close one eye, the world does not look flat. One of the other functions that help us see the world in three dimensions is known as motion parallax. It makes objects farther away seem to move more slowly. The perception of depth through the observation of motion is a very complicated process. But we know that infants can tell the difference between directions of motion as early as seven weeks, and this starts to show up on visual evoked potentials from 10 weeks.

The texture of an object also helps us perceive depth. In many instances texture or pattern is a better cue to depth than motion. Textures that look smaller must be farther away. Infants can see differences in patterns from a very early age. In fact, they have the ability to detect the orientation of lines from birth and can separate areas with different texture patterns from about 12 weeks of age.

Motion parallax enables us to see the world in depth. The BLUE arrows indicate the direction of the cyclist's movement. As the cyclist moves forward, objects are displaced and seem to move in relation to her. The rate of displacement is shown by the thickness of the RED arrows—the thicker arrows indicate that the closer objects appear to move more quickly than the distant ones.

Orientation

The relative position or direction of something.

center-occluded
object

complete
object

fragmented
object

Three views of the same object. Experiments on four-month-old infants suggest they can deduce that a partially covered object is a single unit when it is moving but, unlike adults, not when it is stationary.

Motion and visual occlusion

In 1983, using a preferential looking technique, Philip Kelman and Elizabeth Spelke showed four-month-old infants an object of which the top and bottom were visible, but the center was covered by another, closer object. The infants were shown this display over and over again. They were then shown two new stimuli. One was a complete object, and the other was two fragments of an object. The infants were expected to look longer at the stimuli they believed to be novel. If they perceived the occluded (partially covered) object as one continuous object, they would look more at the fragmented stimuli. However, if they perceived the occluded object as two separate objects, they would look longer at the complete stimuli.

Kelman and Spelke found that when the visible parts of an occluded object moved together behind what was obscuring them, infants perceived them as a single, continuous object, as an adult would. Unlike adults, however, if the occluded object did not move, the findings implied that the infants perceived two separate objects. These findings provide further evidence that infants can use motion as a clue to whether an occluded object is a single unit.

Motion also seems to influence three- to five-month-old infants' perceptions of object boundaries. In one study, infants perceived two overlapping objects as distinct if they moved independently of each other even if they sometimes touched each other while in motion. Yet stationary, overlapping objects were not perceived as separate even if they differed in color, texture, or shape.

Face perception

Faces play an important part in human social interaction. We can show we are happy or angry simply by changing our facial expressions. It is easy to recognize people simply by looking at their faces.

Infants soon learn to distinguish their mother's face from others. From as early as two weeks of age they can watch an adult's face and imitate certain gestures such as sticking out the tongue.

Many researchers believe that young infants' ability to track faces casts significant light on the development of the brain. Although there is a lot of evidence to suggest that it takes infants about three months to learn the layout of facial features, some studies seem to indicate that infants can track facelike stimuli in the first 10 minutes of life. At between four and six weeks old, however, the preferential tracking of faces decreases rapidly. It returns only during the third month of life. This may show that newborns process faces using a different part of the brain from that which they will use for the same operation in later life. If this supposition is correct, it would appear that the cortex (outer layer) of the brain has matured by the time the infant is three months old. Before that other parts of the brain are used for identification.

Curriculum Context

Students should understand that the evolutionary older parts of the brain and the cortex sometimes overlap in their functions.

Externality effect

How do infants recognize familiar faces? Research suggests that newborns can discriminate between two similar faces on the basis of hair, eyes, and mouth. However, if a swimming cap is placed over the two heads on display, infants cannot tell the difference between them until they are about three months old.

The inability to tell the difference between changes in features if a border is placed around them is a product of what is known as the externality effect. If the face has a dynamic expression, such as a smile, the externality effect is reduced.

Emotional expressions

Infants can begin to notice the difference in facial expressions at between four and ten months. They can

Visual Illusions

Visual illusions are one of the most exciting ways to gain insights into how our brains make sense of the world. Most of the time we have no difficulty recognizing objects for what they are, but sometimes we can be fooled. A stick, for example, will appear bent when it is placed in water. This illusion is caused by the process of refraction (bending) of light as it passes from air to water. Similarly, a mirage is caused by light passing through layers of hot air above a heated surface, creating the illusion of a pool of water on desert sands or a highway.

Other illusions occur because of the way our brains process the visual information hitting our eyes. For example, if you stare at a rotating wheel for a minute, then look at a static object, the static object will appear to be spinning, too. This happens because when you fixate on something for a long time, the brain adapts to the stimulus, in this case adaptation to spinning motion. Other visual illusions are sometimes termed cognitive illusions. If you have ever seen an impossible triangle or some of the illustrations by the graphic artist M.C. Escher (1898–1970), you will know how difficult it can

The phenomenon of illusory contour—these lines give the illusion of forming a sphere.

be to make sense of some pictures. Are babies fooled by visual illusions? Can they tell that something is wrong with what they are seeing? There is some evidence to suggest that, even with infants as young as two months, the answer may sometimes be that they can see that it is an illusion. Researchers have shown that infants of different ages can see an illusory contour such as the one shown above, as long as the illusion is stationary.

also see the difference between smiling and laughing expressions. Expressions of emotion are often accompanied by vocalization. For example, a wide-open mouth and eyes may express shock. They are frequently accompanied by a sharp intake of breath. We know that infants can discriminate the vocal sounds of happiness and sadness by three to four months of age and can match them with the appropriate facial expressions. However, what is less clear is whether infants realize that a smiling face and contented sounds mean that the person is "happy."

Social referencing

One way to measure when infants actually understand the meaning of an expression is to observe whether they can adapt their behavior on the basis of other people's emotions. This is known as social referencing. Social referencing can be thought of as the ability to communicate using expressions.

In one experiment, infants and adults are put in an unfamiliar situation. A new toy is brought in. The experimenter tells the adult to make a particular facial expression such as one that conveys happiness or fear. The infant's response to this expression is measured. By about 12 months of age, infants can match their behavior to the emotional expression. So if the mother shows fear when the toy is brought in, the infants avoid it. On the other hand, if the mother's expression is happy, they will approach the toy.

Visual attention

So far we have looked at the development of visual processing. However, much of our understanding of perceptual development has come from measuring infants' attention to visual displays or actions.

In order to attend to an object or event, we have to be alert. During the first month of life, infants are in an alert state for less than 20 percent of the time and sleep for 75 percent of the time. By the age of three months, infants' periods of alertness become more frequent. In young infants before two to three months old, the alert state is achieved mainly by external stimulation—for example, by stroking their faces. However, from 12 weeks of age the ability to maintain attention rather than simply attain it begins to develop.

Curriculum Context

Many curricula expect students to be able to explain what is meant by attention and how it develops in infants.

Attention involves selecting particular objects or events to focus on. Researchers have found that one distinct form of attention is the ability to select and focus on objects no matter where they are located in the visual field. If an object is moved slowly and at a constant speed in one direction in front of a newborn infant, it can follow it with its eyes. However, if the object changes direction or speeds up, then it is no longer able to follow it. This is known as smooth pursuit. By three to four months of age, infants are able to focus on and track faster-moving objects.

During the 1960s and 1970s researchers noticed that before two months of age, infants would fixate on an object for long periods. They took this as evidence that these prolonged fixations meant that infants were not really processing what they were looking at. In other words, they believed that infants were not controlling how long they looked at it. More recently it has been suggested that young infants are unable to disengage their eyes easily.

Disengaging attention

The ability to disengage attention has been measured using overlap-gap tests. In these experiments an object is placed directly in front of an infant's eye. Other target objects are placed so that they overlap the central object, touch it, or are nearby but with a gap in between. The researcher measures the length of time it takes the infants to look at the peripheral targets. Infants have been fastest in shifting their attention when there is a gap, and they are slowest when there is an overlap of the central object and the target objects. This type of study shows that young infants are able to disengage their attention from one object to another.

To test the extent to which an infant can choose not to attend to something, an attractive display is shown while a peripheral stimulus is placed to one side of its

Curriculum Context

Students should be able to discuss the ways scientists measure fixation and disengagement in infants.

Peripheral
Situated on the edge of something.

Visual Cliff

Seeing is much more complicated than simply having eyes to form images of the world around us: We must also understand (perceive) this information. For example, when we walk to the edge of a cliff, we can see that it is a long way to the ground. We easily perceive this depth. But do infants see depth at birth, or do they learn how to see the world in three dimensions?

To put these hypotheses to the test, child psychologist E. J. Gibson asked whether her infant son would stop at a significant drop, or whether he would fall off. In the "visual cliff" experiment an infant is placed on the middle of a glass tabletop. Half of the tabletop rests on a solid tiled box, but the other half stands over a drop to the tiled floor. The aim of the experiment is to see whether infants will avoid crawling over the "cliff." If they do, then this suggests that they can perceive depth without having to learn about it. E. J. Gibson tried this experiment not just with babies, but with young animals as well.

Almost all animals, as soon as they are capable of independent movement, avoided the visual cliff. Goats avoid it from the day they are born. Rats are blind at birth but avoid the cliff as soon as they can see (four weeks). Human infants refuse to crawl over the "cliff" from about seven months of age. Because infants younger than this cannot crawl, it was thought until fairly recently that they did not mind being placed on the transparent table. However, it has since been found that when three-month-old infants are placed on the part of the table above the apparent drop, their heart rate increases, and they open their eyes wide, as if they are scared.

field of vision so that it cannot look at it without taking its eyes off the main object. Researchers found that infants could learn not to look at the peripheral target. In fact, six-month-old infants are able to delay looking at the peripheral target for up to five seconds in order to look at an attractive display in a different location. This suggests that by four to six months of age infants are able to control where they look and where they do not look. Other research has shown that there are three periods of development of visual attention during infancy. From birth until about two months of age infants become more alert and aware of what is going on around them. From two or three months until about six months there is rapid development in spatial orientation. From about five to six months onward infants are able to control their attention.

Auditory perception

Newborns can hear much better than they can see, and therefore it is likely that, for them, auditory perception is at least as important as sight. One of the first sounds that infants hear is their mother's voice. Research in the 1980s showed that infants could discriminate their mother's voice from that of a stranger within one to two days of birth. Are they very quick learners, or might infants be able to recognize their mother's voice while still in the womb?

To answer this question, psychologists ran a study in which they asked pregnant women to read a story aloud to their unborn child twice a day for the last six weeks of pregnancy. When the newborns were two days old, they were read the old story and a new one. The infants sucked more on a teat when they heard the old story than when they heard the new one. This indicates that infants are able to experience and learn some things before they are born.

In 1983 Patricia Kuhl tested children as young as 18 weeks of age to see if they could distinguish contrasting

A mother and daughter read a book together. It is thought that infants hear and learn their mother's voice even before they are born. People are probably also born with some sort of genetically inherited mechanism for recognizing speechlike sounds.

vowel sounds. The subjects of her experiment looked at two identical faces that silently articulated different vowel sounds—"ee" as in "reef" and "o" as in "bob"—while only one of those sounds was played through a speaker. The infants looked significantly longer at the faces that were making the mouth shape compatible with the sound. This result tends to confirm that people are born with some genetically endowed mechanism for registering speechlike sounds. It is this ability to differentiate phonemes that enables children to quickly learn the language to which they are most exposed in infancy.

In 1984 Janet Werker and Richard Tees found that between the ages of six to eight months, infants born of English-speaking parents could discriminate contrasting consonants in Hindi. By the time they were 12 months old, however, these same infants failed to discriminate between the same sounds. This suggests that people are born with some innate mechanism for learning language. Early on, infants can discriminate between all of the speech sounds in the world. However, without exposure to these sounds in the environment, infants will lose this ability and be able to distinguish only between relevant speech sounds in the language they hear around them.

Intersensory integration

In 1984 Elizabeth Spelke showed four-month-old infants two animated cartoon films simultaneously on separate screens. Each film had a soundtrack associated with it. While the infants were watching the films, one of the soundtracks was played on a loudspeaker placed centrally between the two screens. The infants would turn and look significantly longer at a film when the corresponding soundtrack was being played. This suggests that by four months of age infants are learning to integrate and coordinate sensory information from different sources.

Articulated

Formed clearly and distinctly.

Curriculum Context

Students should analyze the role sound recognition plays in language acquisition.

Stages of Development

Two of the most important theories of intellectual, or cognitive, development in children—how a child's thinking changes and develops from infancy to adulthood—were proposed by Lev Vygotsky (1896–1934) and Jean Piaget (1896–1980). Piaget's work in particular has been hugely influential.

Vygotsky proposed that any mental function, such as thought or language, appears twice in the course of development. The first time, a mental function appears outside the child. That is when children are presented with cultural tools, such as words or problem-solving strategies. When they initially use a function, the tool is not quite theirs yet. Over a period of time, however, they will use the tool over and over and again. Through routine and practice they will gradually internalize the tool and make it their own. The stage model proposed by Vygotsky charts the progression of this process of internalization. Because he believed that language and thinking start off as separate mental activities, Vygotsky proposed different stages for them.

Internalize

To incorporate something within the self, either consciously or subconsciously, as a guiding principle.

The development of language

According to Vygotsky, language goes through four stages of development. From birth to about the age of two, children are in the primitive stage. Its essential quality is its lack of intellectual function (that is, it does not involve thinking). Language begins with emotional releases, such as crying or cooing. They are followed by sounds for social reactions, such as

The first stage of language development was defined by Vygotsky as primitive. Before the age of two years old a baby learns to identify the word "milk" with the white liquid he is given to satisfy hunger, but it does not have any independent meaning in the baby's mind.

laughter. The first words emerge as substitutes for objects or desires. The words are merely a conditioned response and have no meaning in their minds yet.

The second stage of language development happens at about the age of two. Children at this stage show a remarkable increase in vocabulary, mostly because they actively ask to be told the names of things. They begin to understand the symbolic value of words and what they represent. This stage is called naive because, although children make grammatically correct sentences, they do not yet understand the underlying structure of language.

Curriculum Context

Students should appreciate the role of grammar in language systems.

The third stage of language development is called egocentric speech and emerges around the age of four. It is called egocentric because most of the speech is not addressed to anyone else. Rather, children perform monologues with themselves, often using different tones of voice as they "act out" different ideas.

Egocentric

Thinking only of oneself without regard for the feelings of others.

Speech influences children's thinking, which in turn influences their speech. This interaction marks the emergence of verbal thought, which allows the child to plan a solution while solving a problem.

The fourth and final stage of a person's language development is the ingrowth stage. The child develops an internalized form of egocentric speech. The sounds of speech are replaced by mental symbols that serve a similar purpose to verbal thought or problem solving. At the same time, the functions of thinking and language become inseparable. Thinking becomes a form of inner speech, and at the same time inner language develops into a form of thinking.

The development of thought
Vygotsky believed that the development of thinking goes through three distinct stages. In the first stage,

children think in unorganized categories. The representations children initially form are trial-and-error groupings. Progressively, a child begins to notice that some events happen at the same time as others. Thought is a social or cultural event: for example, the child begins to associate the appearance of a parent with being cuddled. By the end of the first stage, children are dissatisfied with their categories.

The second stage in thought development is termed "thinking in complexes"—coherent bases for categorizing objects or events. At first, complexes are based on any relationship children notice between objects or events. They then begin to use collection complexes based on contrasts rather than similarity.

In the third stage, conceptual thinking, objects and events can be represented based on abstract properties, such as being able to recognize a shape or pattern in a series of dots. Children analyze and synthesize information in more sophisticated ways. Language plays an important role in this achievement. Words can guide or shape thinking, and the results of thought can be expressed through language.

The role of play and tutors

According to Vygotsky, play is one of the two most important ways to stimulate development. Egocentric speech during play allows children to guide their activities and also helps them internalize speech and make it a sophisticated mental tool. For Vygotsky, playing takes place in the Zone of Proximal Development (ZPD) and involves activities that go beyond children's current levels of development and toward their potential level.

The other important way in which development can be stimulated is through joint activity with a more developed person, such as an older child or an adult.

Conceptual

Based on mental concepts, or ideas.

Synthesize

Combine several things into a coherent whole.

Curriculum Context

Many curricula expect students to contrast Vygotsky's ideas about collaborative learning with other more individualistic theories.

Children at the same level of development cannot stimulate one another through the ZPD. It is a trial-and-error process because they have yet to learn the tools that will take them to a higher level of development.

Older children and adults, on the other hand, have usually mastered (and internalized) the tools that lie within younger children's ZPD. It is thus easier for them to provide the sort of stimulation that will help

The Zone of Proximal Development

Vygotsky was interested in the way development could be stimulated, and he raised the following problem: Suppose two children perform identically on a test; have they achieved the same level of development?

The answer, Vygotsky found, is "no." Imagine Peter and Robert, who are both eight years old. They both take a problem-solving test, and their mental age is calculated to be eight years. We could conclude that Peter and Robert are equally developed. But suppose Peter and Robert are tested again with an adult to help them identify the important features of the problem. With adult help Peter achieves a mental age of nine, while Robert achieves a mental age of eleven.

From tests like this, Vygotsky made a crucial distinction between actual development (what the child can do on her own) and potential development (what the child could do with the help of someone with more expertise). The

The ZPD, shown here in two children, is the difference between what a child can achieve alone and what a child can achieve with help.

diagram shows this difference. Although Peter and Robert achieve similar performances on their own, Robert benefits substantially more from the help of an expert. The term that Vygotsky gave to this area between the actual and the potential level of development was the "zone of proximal development" (ZPD).

Vygotsky suggested that development takes place by stimulation of the ZPD. That is, children develop when they are stimulated beyond their current level of performance. ZPD has an upper limit, though. Stimulation must exceed the child's current development level, but be less than the child's potential level of development.

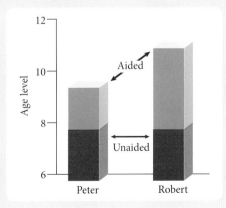

younger children progress from their current level of development and develop new skills that they will eventually internalize.

Evaluation of Vygotsky's work

Vygotsky stressed the influence of culture on development. Children are raised in a social environment that provides pressures as well as an array of cognitive tools, the most important being language. Vygotsky also identified the important difference between actual development, as measured by performance tests, and potential development, as measured with aided performance.

Piaget's developmental theory

Jean Piaget formulated the most ambitious theory of intellectual development that has ever been devised. His theory of cognitive development goes through four distinct stages. Each stage represents a particular organization of all thoughts in a unified mental structure, and each stage also applies to all possible cognitive activities.

Newborns begin to interact with their environment in what Piaget called the sensorimotor stage, which covers the period between birth and two years. The next stage is preoperational thought, which lasts from roughly two to seven years of age. Children at this stage acquire the ability to represent objects and events with symbols, but are incapable of logical thought. They achieve this ability at the next stage, concrete operations. At this stage children can apply logical

Piaget labeled the first period of cognitive development in a child's life the sensorimotor stage. It occurs between birth and two years. Young babies, like the one shown here, begin to develop an awareness of the world around them and to interact with the environment in which they live.

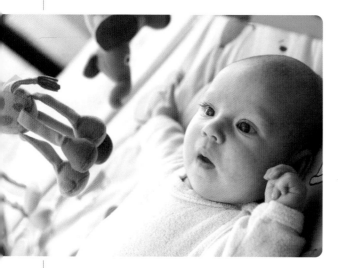

thought to their representations of the external world, but only in the presence of observable objects. This stage lasts from approximately 7 to 11 years. In the final stage, formal operations, children are able to apply logical thought to ideas, not just things. This can give rise to abstract representations, such as justice. The formal operations stage begins roughly around the age of 11 and is usually established by adulthood. Piaget also identified various substages within these four main stages of development.

The sensorimotor stage

Substage one, the refinement of reflexes, occurs between birth and the age of one month. Newborns come into the world with a set of simple reflexes. They suck when objects are placed to their lips or in their mouths (the sucking reflex). If one of their cheeks is touched, they will turn their heads to that side (the rooting reflex). They close their fingers around objects that touch the palm of their hands (the grasping reflex). These reflexes serve useful purposes and are essential for the baby to survive.

During babies' first month outside the womb their sucking becomes more discriminating. Similar changes take place with the grasping reflex, as newborns experience a variety of objects through touching. By sampling the environment, infants develop behaviors that progressively become more adapted to the various forms of stimulation available.

Substage two, the primary circular reactions substage, occurs between the ages of one to four months. The term "circular reactions" refers to the repetitive nature of behaviors in this substage. The earlier reflexes can now be combined into more complex behaviors that infants will repeat if they find them rewarding. For example, if infants grab a toy and succeed in bringing it to their mouths to suck, they will try to do it again.

Curriculum Context

It is important for students to understand the stages of development in Piaget's theory.

Reflex

An action performed without conscious thought in response to a stimulus.

This child is six months old. By the age of two she will have learned to differentiate between herself and other objects, and will also be able to think about her actions, rather than just grabbing at toys because it is an enjoyable thing to do.

Substage three comprises secondary circular reactions, which happens at about four to eight months of age. Interesting behaviors are repeated frequently but now involve outcomes other than the infant's own body, and objects from the environment become the focus of interest. For instance, infants may find throwing toys to the ground extremely interesting.

Substage four usually happens between 8 and 12 months, when infants develop coordination and extension of secondary reactions. Infants show increasingly complex behaviors by combining two or more actions in order to achieve a desired goal. A simple example is the removal of an obstacle in order to retrieve another object. For Piaget this signaled the emergence of goal-directed behavior. Infants are now capable of performing some preliminary actions necessary for achieving desired outcomes and have developed a basic ability to plan.

Another important development is the emergence of object permanence. When you close your hand around a small object in front of infants at substage four, they will not act as if the object has disappeared from the Earth. Instead, they will understand that the object is still there and look expectantly at your hand, waiting for it to appear again.

Substage five begins around 12 to 18 months, when children develop tertiary circular reactions. They involve experimenting with objects to explore their properties. For instance, rather than merely throwing toys, infants will observe how different toys behave when thrown. Or maybe an infant will shake the same rattle in different ways to produce different noises. Instead of repeating identical actions, infants perform similar actions repeatedly, varying their actions to produce different outcomes. For infants at this substage it is the novelty factor that is important.

Substage six comprises mental combinations and the emergence of representations, which happens at about 18 to 24 months. Infants progressively internalize actions and sensations in the form of representations. They begin to think not through action but through representations of actions.

The preoperational stage
During the preoperational stage, between two and seven years of age, continued development mainly involves substantial growth in representational ability, the ability to represent objects and events with symbols and signs. Piaget stressed the difference between symbols and signs. Children use symbols as private representations. They are only meaningful to the child, not to other people. Usually symbols are chosen that resemble the objects they represent.

Signs, however, are representations shared by many people. Words are a good example of what Piaget called signs. Signs do not usually resemble the objects they refer to. For example, the word "house" has no resemblance to the structures we call houses. Despite this, signs are more powerful than symbols because they communicate meaning quickly and efficiently. Switching from symbols to signs expands children's ability to obtain useful information from others. But

Curriculum Context

Many curricula expect students to identify the limitations of stage theories of development.

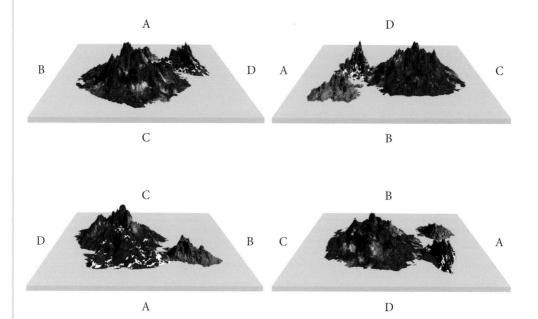

The three mountains test

This test is used to demonstrate egocentricity in preoperational children (two- to four-year-olds). Three papier-mâché mountains, with different shapes, colors, and features, are arranged on a table. The sides of the table are labeled A, B, C, and D. The child being tested explores the model and is then seated on one side of it. A doll is then placed on one of the other sides. The child is shown a series of photographs and asked to choose the one that shows the mountains from the doll's point of view. It is not until the age of seven or eight years that children can "put themselves" in the doll's place.

although preschoolers may use signs such as words, it doesn't follow that they use them in a way that will be meaningful to others.

Over the course of the preoperational period, children learn to see things from other people's viewpoints. This has many advantages, one being that it makes it possible for them to have meaningful conversations with other people.

The concrete operations stage

This stage occurs between the ages of 7 and 11. By "operations" Piaget meant mental routines for processing information in a logical manner. In this stage, operations can form mental representations of how things work, but only in relation to observable phenomena, which is why it is called concrete, as opposed to abstract.

Phenomenon

(plural: phenomena) An observable fact, condition, or event.

The ability to carry out concrete operations increases learning possibilities as children experiment with various object properties at the same time rather than merely exploring single properties. When children experiment with more complex problems, they are not systematic; there is still a large element of trial-and-error, and they often repeat steps.

Formal operations

The ability to think about one's thoughts is often called metacognition. It is the most sophisticated form of thinking and marks the final stage in Piaget's theory of development. With formal operations, from about the age of 11 years onward children are able to think about possible events and not just actual events. This is a significant change. If you can think about the various possible ways to solve a problem, it becomes much easier to plan how you will carry out a task. If you are not bound to the immediately perceptible world, you can entertain some abstract concepts such as justice, freedom, and so forth.

The formal operations stage marks the end of development in Piaget's theory, but it does not mark the end of thinking. In fact, because children are no longer bound to the immediately perceptible world, an infinity of thoughts can be entertained.

Mechanisms of change

Piaget proposed that all the changes during development are controlled by a small set of mechanisms, or processes for achieving particular results. According to Piaget, the basic mechanisms that adapt a child's cognitive structure are assimilation, accommodation, equilibration, and abstraction.

Curriculum Context

Students should appreciate the mechanisms Piaget believed are involved in cognitive development.

When children receive information, it is deformed to fit their current cognitive structure, a process Piaget called assimilation. In the process it becomes distorted. Accommodation is the mechanism that "stretches" the thought structure to accommodate new information.

Equilibrium

Children are in a state of equilibrium when their current thought structure is able to deal with most new experiences. Equilibration, the process by which equilibrium is achieved, allows children's performance to improve. It evaluates the level of distortion generated by assimilation and requests the necessary amount of accommodation to minimize these distortions. Over time the cognitive structure stabilizes in an ideal state. Later, however, the limitations of children's thought structure mean that they fail to solve a variety of problems. The accumulation of failures will create disequilibrium and prompt structural changes that allow the children to move to the next stage.

Abstraction

The progression from one stage to another is made possible through the mechanism of abstraction. Abstraction creates a new cognitive structure that is based on the previous structure, but which attempts, in the process, to correct the limitations that caused disequilibrium in the previous structure. Equilibration ensures that an ideal balance between assimilation and accommodation takes place during this process.

Evaluation of Piaget's theory

Piaget made major contributions to the study of child development. On the subject of child testing he argued that children should be provided with the opportunity to justify their behavior. Piaget's focus was on children's errors, which offer a clearer insight into the underlying thought processes. Piaget devised a wide range of ingenious tasks to study children's reasoning errors. His experiments on object permanence and conservation are classics, and they are easily replicable. Most of his tasks still generate substantial research.

Although Piaget's theory has been a major influence, it has also been severely criticized by psychologists. Many researchers find the definitions of Piaget's mechanisms of change too vague to be of practical use. For many psychologists it isn't clear what assimilation and accommodation are, and equilibration and abstraction prove even more puzzling.

A more severe blow to Piaget's theory is the discovery that some abilities within a stage do not develop at the same rate. Some conservation problems can be solved as early as six years of age, while other problems are only solved later, at around 10 years of age.

Curriculum Context

Students should be aware of objections and alternatives to Piaget's theories of development.

Some Alternatives to Piaget's Theory

Domain-specific theories Some scientists reject Piaget's notion that children's mental skills develop in a single cognitive structure. Instead, they believe that different skills develop in different mental "domains." Researchers have suggested different domains for language, visual perception, mathematical understanding, and so on. Different domains may develop independently of one another—in stages, according to some researchers, continuously, according to others.

Constructivist theory The U.S. psychologist Jerome Bruner proposed that learning is an active social process in which children use their current knowledge to construct new ideas or concepts. Unlike Piaget, Bruner suggested that children's development is accelerated by giving them tasks they are capable of accomplishing, rather than tasks that are beyond them. They build on success, not failure. In tackling new tasks, children use the information they already have to help them go beyond the information given.

Information-processing theories Information-processing theorists use the computer as a model for cognitive development. Like computers, children take in information (the input), encode and store it, and then respond to it by behaviors (the output). Information-processing theorists approach development mainly by studying children's memory. The more complex a problem, the more memory space is required. Young children have limited memory space. As they develop, the amount of memory space increases.

Memory Development

Knowing your own identity is something you take for granted. But have you ever wondered how you know who you are? Does it ever amaze you that this information is always in your memory? Do you sometimes wonder how you came to know yourself? Do young infants know who they are? How does memory develop?

There are three main kinds of memory storage: sensory memory, short-term memory (also termed working memory), and long-term memory. Sensory memory describes the effects of stimulation on senses such as vision, hearing, touch, taste, and smell.

Short-term memory

When you pay attention to a stimulus—that is, when you become conscious of it—it becomes part of short-term memory. Short-term memory is what we are immediately aware of at any given time. Keeping things in mind for a short period is necessary for thinking and understanding. That is why short-term memory is often known as working memory. Short-term memory is severely limited: Its effects last for seconds, and in adults it is limited to about seven items.

Curriculum Context

Many curricula expect students to demonstrate the role imagery plays in encoding.

"The lizard's name is Adolphus." If this sentence were very important to you and you desperately wanted to remember it, you might reread it and repeat it to yourself several times. This process is known as rehearsing. Alternatively, you might make a mental link between some Adolphus you know and this lizard, a process termed elaborating. Or you might think of some other meaningful way of remembering the sentence by organizing it with other items of information you possess. Rehearsing, elaborating, and organizing are the three most important strategies we have for bringing information from short-term to long-term memory, a process known as encoding.

Learning to ride a bike uses implicit rather than explicit memory. This means that this girl will be able to learn by doing, but she will not be able to describe or explain exactly what she is doing to another person.

Long-term memory

Long-term memory contains our relatively permanent information about the world. It includes everything we know about ourselves, about others, and about things. It represents the long-term effects of all the experiences we have had. Some of this information is explicit: It can be put into words. And some of it is implicit: It cannot be put into words. Implicit memory is also called nondeclarative memory because it consists of memories that are nonverbalizable, for example, skills such as walking or tying shoelaces. There are two types of explicit memory, and they seem to involve different parts of the brain. Semantic memory consists of abstract information like the facts you learn at

K. C.'s Memories

A patient of the psychologist Endel Tulving identified only as K. C. went to him as part of his rehabilitation after a motorcycle accident that left him with serious brain damage. Despite his injuries, K. C. seemed a bright, alert, and quite normal young man. He appeared to remember everything he had ever learned. He knew how to play chess, where he lived, what he owned, multiplication tables, and a host of other abstract facts, the things that make up what we define as semantic memory or abstract information.

But Tulving soon discovered that although K. C.'s semantic memory was intact, his episodic memory or recollection of personal experiences (also called autobiographical memory) seemed to have vanished completely. For example, although K. C. was certain that his parents had a cottage, and knew exactly where it was and everything that was in it, he could not remember a single time that he had ever been there. Similarly, although he knew how to play chess, he had no specific memory of the time, place, or people present when he had played a match. The case of K. C. provides strong evidence that different parts of the brain are involved in semantic (abstract) and episodic (autobiographical) memory.

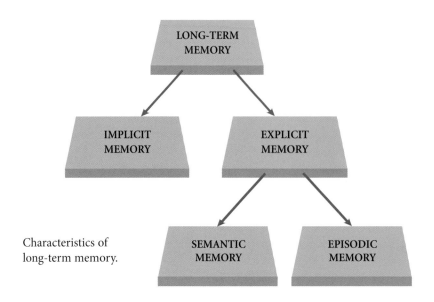

Characteristics of long-term memory.

school such as addition or multiplication. Episodic memory consists of the memories that make up your recollection of your personal experiences.

Our long-term memories are extremely important to our sense of who we are. All of our skills, our habits, our competence, our very identity reside in long-term memory. Patients who suffer memory loss may eventually lose even the most basic competence required for the tasks of daily life.

Curriculum Context

It is useful for students to list examples that distinguish between episodic, semantic, implicit, and explicit memory.

Memory in infants

Because young infants cannot put their memories into words, investigators have devised ways of studying how experiences affect them and what they remember. Researchers measure something known as the orienting response. People make an orienting response when there is new stimulation. Heart rate slows down, pupils increase in size, and skin becomes more conductive to electricity as a result of very subtle increases in perspiration. The usefulness of this for the psychologist lies in the fact that whenever a stimulus is no longer novel—in other words, when it has been learned and is therefore remembered—the orienting response stops happening.

Imitation

Infants' ability to imitate provides another way of studying memory. The argument is that if infants imitate an action, that is evidence that they can remember it. In a number of studies people bend over infants' cribs and purse their lips, stick out their tongues, or blink their eyes. In some studies, investigators report that within an hour of birth some infants respond by blinking, sticking out their tongues, or pursing their lips. But it is not entirely clear that infants are actually imitating. It is possible that sticking out the tongue and pursing the lips are simply reflexive (automatic) behaviors brought about by the closeness of the person.

Controlled behaviors

With older infants it is possible to study memory by looking at behaviors that the infant can control. The most common approach to testing the memory of a human or monkey infant is the "the delayed nonmatch to sample procedure," in which the investigator shows infants a sample object—say, a small box. When the infants reach for the box, a reward is presented. The box is then taken away and later presented again, along with a second, different object—say, a teddy bear. Now the infants are rewarded only if they reach for the new object. The procedure continues for a number of trials with a variety of novel objects being paired with the original object. The infants are rewarded only when they reach for the novel object, not the original one.

This task requires at least three capabilities: learning and remembering a rule (the new object is always the one that is rewarded), remembering which object is familiar in order to identify the new one, and being able to reach in an intended direction. Infant monkeys do not usually accomplish these three tasks until they are at least four months old. Human infants, who

Curriculum Context

Students could usefully analyze memory studies on animals to compare human and animal memories.

develop more slowly than apes, rarely perform very well until they are at least a year old.

A-not-B

The A-not-B experiment gives an indication of the age at which infants develop short-term memory. If you show an object—say, a ring—to four- or five-month-old infants and then hide it under a pillow (which we will call pillow A) while they are watching, they will have no difficulty reaching for and retrieving it.

Now suppose that after you have hidden the ring under pillow A, you remove it and slip it under a second pillow (B) right next to it, again in full view of an infant. The infant reaches for A, not B. It is not until after the age of eight months or so that infants reliably reach toward B. But if there is a delay of as little as 8 seconds between hiding the object and letting the infant retrieve it, very few infants less than a year old will reach for it under pillow B.

Early brain development

The infant's brain grows very rapidly during the first two years of life. This growth involves the growth of protective coatings over brain cells and the development of a vast number of connections between existing nerve cells. In fact, the brain of a two-year-old may contain more potential connections than it ever will again. That is because many of the billions of connections that are not used eventually disappear—a process that is known as neural (nerve cell) pruning.

The infant's brain consists of three main parts: the brain stem (at the lower rear of the brain, like an extension of the spinal cord); the cerebellum, which is also at the lower rear of the brain, behind the brain stem; and the cerebrum—the wrinkled, grayish-looking mass that you see if a human skull is opened from the top.

The brain stem and other lower parts of the brain are more highly developed and functional in the infant—and in the fetus—than are the structures of the cerebrum. That is because the brain stem is closely involved in physiological activities such as breathing, heart functioning, and digestion. Hence it is essential for physical survival. The cerebrum is more concerned with activity of the senses, movement, and balance. Some of its most important functions relate to thinking, language, and speech.

Not surprisingly, an infant's memory appears to be closely tied to the development and functioning of different parts of the brain. Charles Nelson suggests that the infant's first memories, which cannot be put into words and are therefore said to be implicit (or preexplicit), depend on lower brain structures such as the brain stem and the cerebellum. These structures, as we saw, are the most highly developed at birth. The infant's more explicit memories begin to appear toward the end of the first year of life. These memories are more dependent on the structures of the cerebrum.

Curriculum Context

Students should understand which parts of the brain are involved in memory.

Memory in young infants

Within a few days of birth, infants are able to recognize their mother's voice as well as her smell. Studies have found that infants turn more readily toward the sound of their mother's voice than anyone else's. Similarly, they react more positively to smells associated with their mothers than to smells associated with others. But while this is clear evidence of memory, it may be memory of information acquired before birth rather than from postnatal learning.

Curriculum Context

Students should consider the evidence that suggests babies have memories from before they were born.

The infant's first implicit memories are fleeting recollections, not long remembered—unless, of course, there are reminders between learning and being asked to remember. For example, infants can quite easily learn an association between a puff of air and a musical tone. A puff of air blown into infants' eyes causes them to blink. If the puff of air is blown into their eyes a number of times, and if it is always preceded by the distinctive sound of a single piano note, the infants will quickly learn to blink whenever they hear the note. They will continue to react in this way even when there is no longer a puff of air directed at their eyes. This is an example of a kind of learning known as conditioning.

The interesting thing about this kind of learning in early infancy is that the infants may show evidence of remembering. In this instance, infants continued to

Infantile Amnesia

By the age of two the infant's long-term memory is nothing short of astonishing compared to what it was earlier in the first year of life. But they will be able to tell you nothing about any of their personal experiences throughout infancy and even through most of the early preschool period.

This curious phenomenon, known as infantile amnesia, is so powerful that when researchers showed 9- and 10-year-old children photographs

of their classmates from their early preschool years, they were unable to recognize them. Yet when adults were shown photographs of their elementary school classmates, they recognized more than 90 percent of them. It made no difference that many of these adults had been out of school for more than half a century.

No one knows for certain why we are subject to infantile amnesia. One theory is that structures of the brain involved in long-term, autobiographical (episodic) memory are not sufficiently developed during this period. Another theory is that the child has not yet developed the kinds of memory strategies that are required. Yet another theory is that the infant does not have a sufficiently strong sense of self with which to associate autobiographical memories.

This lady can tell her daughter about many people from her youth. At the age of 10, however, she would not have been able to remember the preschoolers she was with every day.

blink in response to the tone on the following day, for a half-dozen days afterward, or sometimes even longer.

Changes in infant memory

Child psychologist Marion Perlmutter describes three stages in the development of infant memories. The first spans the first three months of the infant's life. As we have seen, during this period infant memories appear to result mainly from the repeated pairing of events, such as the presence of the mother and her voice or smell. These memories represent a very simple kind of learning. And most strikingly, the young infant's memory during these months is often fleeting and highly impermanent. Memory during this period seems to be largely a matter of neurons firing when a new stimulus is presented and then stopping when the stimulus becomes more familiar.

Neurons
Brain cells specialized to conduct nerve impulses.

The second stage in infant memory development begins at the age of about three months. It is marked by two things: recognition of familiar objects and events, and the beginnings of intentional behaviors. As infants grow older, objects and events become progressively more familiar. As a result the time needed for habituation to these more familiar objects and events continues to shorten. This is evidence that the infants are learning and remembering, and, as a result, can recognize things that are familiar. Soon infants begin to look and search actively for objects and people. Repeatedly reaching for a recognized object or person is proof of intentional or directed behaviors, as opposed to behaviors that are primarily accidental or random.

Habituation
The process of becoming familiar and disinterested.

During the third of Perlmutter's stages, which begins at the age of about eight months, infants' memories have become more like those of adults. They are more abstract and symbolic. Infants can now pay attention and try to remember things. A one-year-old can not only readily recognize members of the family such as their mother or father or the family pet, but can also associate each of them, and dozens of other things, with a whole repertoire of remembered feelings and impressions—perhaps even words.

Memory in younger children

Between ages two and six, children learn at an amazing rate. This is especially evident in the acquisition of language, where there is an enormous growth in vocabulary. This vocabulary spurt begins toward the last half of the infant's second year of life and continues into the preschool period. So good are children at learning words during this period that very often only one or two exposures to a new word are sufficient to ensure that they will be able to remember and use that particular word during the rest of their lives.

The Reliability of Child Witnesses

How can you, a devious and smart prosecutor, make a preschool child remember and help you nail your prime suspect?

Well, you should ask leading questions such as "Did the man have a beard?" rather than open-ended questions like "Tell me what the man looked like." You should ask your leading question repeatedly and on different days. It might not hurt if you also use emotional inducement. Try saying things like: "That man has done a lot of bad things, and you can help us get him!"

Using these methods, you may well be highly successful in getting your preschool witnesses to misremember and wrongly accuse someone. You may be guilty of planting false memories—memories for things that never happened. This is especially true when considered in the light of the following research findings about preschoolers:

- They are less likely than older children and adults to correctly identify a guilty person.
- They are more likely than older children or adults to mistakenly identify an innocent person as being guilty.
- They can be made, by the power of suggestion, to remember events that never occurred.
- When asked to imagine something, they may later report the imagined event as though it actually happened.
- Preschoolers have a "yes" response bias. They are more likely to say that something happened rather than that it didn't or even to admit that they do not know.
- When preschoolers are asked to guess repeatedly, they become progressively more certain of their guesses, often ending up totally confident that the guess is the truth.

Nevertheless, there are some important differences between the memories of preschoolers and those of older children and adults. Most noticeably, preschoolers do not use the powerful memory strategies that older children and adults use: organizing, rehearsing, and elaborating. They have not yet developed notions of themselves as learners and rememberers, and they have not figured out that certain strategies can make it a lot easier to remember.

Although many preschoolers seem able to use strategies for remembering, very few do so spontaneously. For example, when three-year-olds were asked to bury a toy in a large sandbox, only about one in five thought of marking the spot so they could find it later, even though they were asked if there was anything else they wanted to do before leaving. However, half of a second group who were instructed to try to remember where the toy was hidden used the simple strategy of marking the spot.

Memory in older children

When researchers asked the mothers of four-year-olds to help their children learn and remember different things, most of the mothers spontaneously used strategies with their children. Children may learn to use memory strategies partly from these sorts of social interactions. It is clear that children become better memorizers as they age at least partly because they make more and better use of strategies.

Improvements in memory are clearly related to children's increasing use of strategies such as organizing and rehearsing. They are also closely linked to increasing familiarity with things and events. In studies in which children are shown photographs depicting different scenes, the more familiar the children are with the scenes, the better they can remember details from the pictures.

Curriculum Context

Many curricula expect students to investigate the strategies children use to aid memory.

Development of Problem Solving

Problem solving is a term used by psychologists to describe the ability of an individual to deal with a situation of some complexity that demands initiative and mental agility if a certain goal is to be reached. The reasoning processes that people bring to problem solving cast light on the nature of intelligence.

Problem solving is a means of finding a way to achieve an objective that is not immediately attainable. As children grow older, they become increasingly able to solve complex problems.

Two theories of development

According to Jean Piaget (1896–1980), children's problem-solving abilities develop in clearly defined stages. Their skills both reflect and are appropriate to the stage of development they have reached. Children have their own strategies and will solve certain types of problem only when they are ready to do so. However, some information-processing theorists regard problem-solving development as a more gradual and continuous process linked to increasing powers of memory. They focus on how children represent problems, the processes they use to solve them, and the way these processes change as the children's memories improve.

The scale of the problem

One fundamental aspect of problem solving is the ability to use symbols such as mental images, language, and numbers to represent real objects. Although Piaget thought that children could not use representations before the age of about 18 months, subsequent research has shown that even infants under one year of age may use gestures to stand for various objects or events.

Nevertheless, older infants and children are much better at using symbols to help them solve problems.

In an experiment conducted in 1987 by Judy Deloache, two- and three-year-old children were asked to search for a toy in a scale model of a room. Later the children were taken into a life-size room just like the model they had seen. When asked to find the toy, the three-year-olds were successful in more than 70 percent of trials because they tended to look where they had found the toy in the scale model. Two-year-olds were successful in only about 20 percent of trials. The difference could not be explained in terms of poorer memory among the two-year-olds because when both age groups went back to the scale model, they were equally successful at locating the toy. It seems that two-year-olds have difficulty in understanding that a scale model can represent a life-size room, but that by age three this understanding has developed.

Preschool children still have difficulty using symbols and numbers that do not refer to real objects. Many experiments have shown that children between the ages of three and five can solve simple arithmetical problems if the numbers are small and related to real things. For example, questions such as: "If there are three children in a candy store, and two go out, how

Toddlers such as this one make no discernible distinction between reality and fantasy, toy railroads and prototype trains. But by about the age of three, children can understand that a symbol or model can represent a real object or situation.

many children are left in the shop?" are easier to answer than: "What does one and two make?"

Planning

Planning is another important aspect of problem solving. However, it can be quite demanding and carries the risk that the effort may be wasted if the child fails to execute the plan correctly. Another drawback is that planning requires inhibiting the tendency to act immediately, an ability that develops slowly over the course of childhood.

Despite these complications, it seems that children often do plan from a very early age. The following experiment with two groups of 12-month-old infants was carried out by Peter Willatts. Each group was seated at a table. On the table was a small barrier, and beyond that was a cloth. For one group of infants, one end of a length of string was placed on the cloth, and the other end was attached to a toy at the far end of the table. The setup for the other group of infants was almost identical, except that the string was not attached to the toy. The first group of children tended to remove the barrier, pull the cloth toward them, grab the string, and pull it to reach the toy. Children in the second group tended to play with the barrier, were slower to reach for the cloth, and did not pull the string. This suggested they realized the string was not attached and could not help them reach the toy.

Goals and subgoals

Successful task completion in the first group involves comparing the current state with the goal state and finding the action that will bring the two together. Because the string is initially out of the children's reach, the children set the subgoal of bringing it closer; that is achieved by moving the cloth. Yet even this action is not immediately possible because of the barrier, so the removal of the barrier becomes another subgoal.

Curriculum Context

Students may be asked to look for examples of creative thinking in problem solving.

The setting of goals and subgoals in order to reduce the difference between the current state and the goal state is a form of planning known as means-ends analysis. Willatts found that the rudiments of means-ends analysis are present in children as young as four months old. As children grow up, the number and complexity of subgoals they can keep in mind

Monkey Cans

In the standard version of the Tower of Hanoi puzzle there are three pegs. On the first peg are 64 disks of decreasing sizes, with the largest at the bottom and the smallest at the top. The other two pegs are empty. The task is to move all the disks until they are in the same arrangement on the third peg. They can be moved only one at a time, and a larger disk cannot be placed on top of a smaller one.

In 1981 David Klahr and Mitch Robinson of Carnegie-Mellon University developed a version of the Tower of Hanoi better suited to children in which the rings were replaced with cans of different sizes, and the rule was that smaller cans could not be placed over larger cans. To make the task fun, it was described in the form of a story about monkeys, hence the name "Monkey Cans." The cans represented a mommy, a daddy, and a baby monkey who can jump from tree to tree.

To help the children keep in mind the goal of the task, the desired arrangement of cans and pegs was set up in front of them. Instead of

actually moving the cans, the children had to tell the researchers their sequence of moves. In this way the researchers could establish the extent to which the children planned their moves. The researchers also varied the number of cans and where they were placed at the start of the task.

Klahr and Robinson found that most four-year-olds were able to find the best solution to two-move puzzles, but not to more complicated problems. Five- and six-year-olds were good on four-move problems, and most six-year-olds could solve six-move problems.

It seems that the difference in abilities shown by the younger and older children is simply one of degree: Young children try to plan ahead, but sometimes forget the objectives, while older children are able to hold more information in mind and so can plan further ahead.

The front row of pegs is the model that the children are asked to reproduce on the back row without placing smaller cans over larger ones.

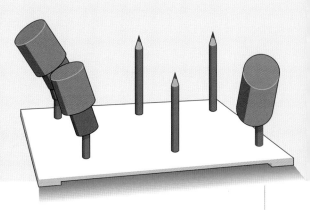

increases along with their ability to resist the lure of short-term goals that divert them from longer-term objectives. These developments are associated with a greater ability to implement means-ends strategy.

Causal judgments

Problem solving often involves trying to understand what caused a particular event. Causal judgments are based on three main principles. First, the assumption that when two events occur close to each other in time and space, the second has been caused by the first. This is known as the contiguity principle. Second, the idea that all causes happen before their effects—this is termed the precedence principle. Third is the covariation principle, which is based on the assumption that if a certain cause has produced a particular effect on a previous occasion, it will do so again.

Curriculum Context

Many curricula expect students to understand the principles behind the causes of events.

Awareness of contiguity

Modern research has shown that even in the first year of life babies are sensitive to contiguity in time and space. Six- to ten-month-old infants spend longer looking at scenes that violate the contiguity principle than at scenes that are consistent with it. The precedence principle (cause precedes effect) seems to be in place with most children by about age three. When we need to discover which of several possible causes is the true cause of an effect, we must observe which of the possible causes occurs regularly and predictably with the effect. This ability—the covariation principle—also seems to develop by three or four years of age.

Use of analogy

Another problem-solving mechanism that develops in children is the ability to reason analogically. To do this, children need to find correspondences between the familiar and the new problems.

Analogically

Using knowledge about past situations to deal with new ones.

Evidence for Transitive Reasoning in Young Children

In 1990 Rosalind Pears and Peter Bryant tested preschool children of various ages to find out if they were able to make transitive inferences. Transitive inference is the ability to deduce a relationship from a series of relationships that were learned separately. Children were presented with pairs of differently colored bricks in little towers of two. Then, using single bricks, the children had to build a larger tower by adding bricks in the order that matched the relationships between the bricks in the little towers.

On some trials the children were asked to build a tower of four bricks. On others they had to build a tower of five bricks, and on a third set they had to build a tower of six bricks.

Before building the tower, the children were asked a series of questions requiring transitive inferences, such as: "Which will be the higher in the tower that you are going to build, the green brick or the blue one?" The children performed significantly above chance on two-thirds of the questions, suggesting that the ability to make transitive inferences is in place at the age of four.

Diagram representing the transitive inference task used by Pears and Bryant. Children are shown pairs of bricks (1); the children are then given single bricks to build a tower (2). Before building the tower, they are asked about the relative positions of bricks within the tower (3); the child builds the tower (4).

Karen Singer Freeman showed that two-year-old children can reason analogically. She devised problems involving the causal relations of stretching, fixing, opening, rolling, breaking, and attaching. In one test, children were given a piece of elastic, a toy bird, and a model landscape with a tree at one end and a rock at the other. They were then asked if they could use these materials to make the bird fly.

Before attempting the problem, some, but not all, of the children had watched the experimenter stretch a rubber band between two poles to make a "bridge" across which she then rolled an orange. Of the children who had not seen this demonstration, only 6 percent thought of the stretching solution to the transfer problem. Of those who had seen the demonstration, 28 percent solved the new problem. And when these children were given a hint that the elastic needed to be used, 48 percent found the solution.

Pragmatic reasoning schemas

Deductive reasoning follows logically from the information given. One task that has been widely used to investigate deductive reasoning in both children and adults is the selection task, first developed by Peter Wason in 1966. In the original version, participants were shown four partially obscured items of evidence and asked which of them they would need to look at more closely in order to test a rule. To test the rule, you need to look for cards that could potentially show the rule to be false. Only about 10 percent of people perform this task correctly. But when it is modified to involve a more realistic content, performance improves considerably. Such tasks may activate familiar knowledge structures in the mind. Constructs of this type are known to psychologists as pragmatic reasoning schemas.

Curriculum Context

Students should be able to describe the steps involved in the problem-solving process.

Verbal Syllogism Problems

A syllogism is a form of reasoning in which a third proposition is formed from two initial ones. In 1984 J. Hawkins, R. D. Pea, J. Glick, and S. Scribner gave the following instructions to four- and five-year-old children:

"I am going to read you some little stories. Some of them are about make-believe animals and things, and some of them are about real animals and things. Some of the stories are going to sound sort of funny. I want you to pretend that everything the stories say is true."

Following an initial practice story, the problems were read one at a time to the children. The answers to the problems were either "Yes" or "No." Here are some examples of the problems used:

1. Bears have big teeth.
   Animals with big teeth can't read books.
   Can bears read books?
2. Rabbits never bite.
   Cuddly is a rabbit.
   Does Cuddly bite?
3. Glasses bounce when they fall.
   Everything that bounces is made of rubber.
   Are glasses made of rubber?
4. Every banga is purple.
   Purple animals always sneeze at people.
   Do bangas sneeze at people?
5. Pogs wear blue boots.
   Tom is a pog.
   Does Tom wear blue boots?
6. Merds laugh when they're happy.
   Animals that laugh don't like mushrooms.
   Do merds like mushrooms?

Children averaged 94 percent correct on congruent problems (questions based on what they know, such as 1 and 2), but only 13 percent correct on incongruent problems such as 3, which is contrary to what they know. On the fantasy problems (4–6), where previous knowledge could neither help nor hinder performance, children scored 73 percent on average.

One type of schema is known as the permission schema. Because children encounter many rules about what they may or may not do, they might be expected to reason about rules at quite an early age. Paul Harris and Maria Núñez showed that even three- and four-year-olds can engage in some basic reasoning about permission rules. Most children of this age were able to identify one picture from a set of four that showed a rule being broken. For example, the children were told about a girl named Sally who wants to play outside. Sally's mother tells her: "If you play outside, you must put your coat on." The children were then shown four pictures of Sally: indoors with her coat on, indoors without her coat on, outdoors with her coat on, and outdoors without her coat on. Most children correctly chose the last picture.

Class inclusion

Class inclusion is a logical task that Piaget associated with the concrete operations stage. For example, think of a bunch of flowers that includes four red flowers and two white ones. In Piaget's experiments children would be shown the flowers and asked: "Are there more red flowers or more flowers here?" Children younger than six years of age tended to say that there were more red flowers. For Piaget this was evidence that they could not think simultaneously about the parts and the whole of an entity.

However, the problem with Piaget's question is that it seems to violate the normal conventions for communication. A more natural way of asking the question might be to say: "Are there more red flowers, or are there more flowers in the bunch?" Several studies have shown that five- and six-year-olds (and three- and four-year-olds in one experiment) can correctly answer class-inclusion problems when the question involves familiar collective terms such as "a bunch of flowers" or "a class of children."

"Are there more red flowers or more flowers here?"—the form of words is so weird that any researcher using it is unlikely to elicit the desired response. The wording of questions is important when studying the class-inclusion skills of young children.

Family matters

Usha Goswami suggested that the word "family" is a particularly useful collective noun in this context. Most children are familiar with the term and know that a family is made up of parents and children. Goswami and her colleagues conducted an experiment with four- and five-year-old children who had all failed a standard class-inclusion task. The children were shown a family of toy mice or a family of yo-yos. Next, the children were asked to construct families of two parents and three children from an assortment of toy animals or other types of toy. Following this task, the children were given four class-inclusion problems involving toy frogs, sheep, building blocks, and balloons. The collective nouns "group," "herd," "pile," and "bunch" were used for these problems. Another group of children who had not participated in the "create-a-family" task were given the same problems. The children who had engaged in creating families performed much better on the class-inclusion problems than those who had not.

Curriculum Context

Students may like to consider the effects social factors have on the success of problem solving.

Information processing

According to Piagetian theory, aspects of problem solving that require logical thought should not start to appear in children until seven years of age. Metacognitive understanding should not appear until the age of 11. Yet subsequent research has indicated that the kind of abilities required for problem solving develop at an earlier age than Piaget predicted.

Information-processing theorists argue that the very idea of stages of development is wrong. They believe that development occurs more gradually. As children's working memory capacity expands, they are able to represent more information and think about more complex strategies for problem solving.

Metacognitive

Concerning awareness of one's own thought processes.

Emotional Development

People experience spontaneous emotions, yet they differ from each other in the types of emotions they experience in different contexts and also in how they control these emotional reactions. How do these differences develop? And how does emotional development relate to children's cognitive and social development?

Chronology

The arrangement of events in the order in which they occur.

There are many different theories about the causes of emotional development and different accounts of its chronology. However, insofar as it is possible to generalize, the following landmarks are passed at roughly the following ages.

From birth to two years

Babies show most of their emotions through crying— it is their only method of communication. Other emotions present at this age are distress and disgust. Social smiling begins during this period, together with anger, surprise, and sadness.

Between four and eight months, infants begin to express a wider range of emotions. Pleasure, happiness, fear, and frustration are shown through noises such as gurgles, coos, wails, and cries, and physical movements such as kicking, arm-waving, rocking, and smiling.

At around 18 months, toddlers start to develop a sense of self. They recognize their image in a mirror as themselves and begin to become independent of their mothers or caregivers. Toddlers of around this age often have a broad range of emotional states.

Babies have at least three different cries that caregivers quickly learn to tell apart. The cry most often heard is the one that signals hunger. The other two cries signal anger and pain.

Two years onward

From this age most children are able to communicate their thoughts and feelings in words. Increasingly, emotions can be controlled or repressed and sometimes replaced by moods. A mood is a state of mind and may last for a considerable period. Children quickly learn to control or regulate their emotions. Much of this regulation, particularly in early childhood, occurs through social interaction.

The development of emotions

Emotion is a feeling state that motivates the individual to carry out some sort of action. Emotions are not just language labels that we apply to these feeling states; they contain biological or physiological components: for example, anger and fear are associated with increases in heart rate and blood pressure. Thinking and perception are also involved in emotion. In order to become fearful or angry as a result of some event that has just occurred, we must first notice it, then decide what to do about it, and finally react.

Physiological

Concerning the way living organisms and their body parts work.

Primary emotions

By six months of age, infants are showing evidence of primary emotions—interest, happiness or joy, surprise, sadness, anger, fear, and disgust. Some researchers believe that these distinct emotions emerge over time from the basic emotions of contentment and distress. Others take the view that they are present from the beginning of life, but are not easily distinguished from external signs. It is important to note that because researchers rely solely on the facial expression of these emotions; it is not possible to make any valid distinction between emotions as they are expressed and emotions as they are experienced.

Curriculum Context

Many curricula expect students to be able to list and categorize emotions.

Secondary emotions

More complex emotions emerge during the second year of life. They are known as secondary or social emotions and they include feelings such as shame, guilt, and embarrassment. They emerge as children begin to show clear signs of self-awareness, and their language skills begin to expand. Some toddlers are very compliant because they are sensitive to social emotions, but other toddlers may have little regard for other people's ideas about appropriate behavior.

Emotion regulation

Emotions occur as part of our adaptation to a constantly changing environment. When we are frightened, we may experience rapid heartbeat and a churning stomach. To survive as a species we need these strong internal signals that motivate us to act. However, once the need for this strong signal has passed, we also need a way of regulating these emotions so that we are not always passively responding to everything that happens around us.

If our emotions are well-regulated, we are then able to enjoy social interactions with others, interactions in which we learn new and important skills that allow us to function in complex societies. If our emotions are poorly regulated, it is very difficult to attend to and learn from these interactions with people and objects. Poorly regulated emotions are also central to the emergence of behavioral and emotional problems.

Coregulation of emotions

Infants have a few basic skills for regulating emotions. For example, some infants are able to soothe themselves if they become overstimulated by looking away or by sucking a thumb or fist. However, even with these rudimentary skills, young children still rely on their mothers and fathers to help them regulate their emotional reactions; for example, parents can hold and soothe frightened infants. This shared coregulation of emotions is a central component of the parent–child relationship throughout infancy and childhood. As

Compliant

Inclined to obey rules or agree with others.

Curriculum Context

Students should evaluate the importance of emotion regulation in complex societies.

children acquire language skills, more coregulation of emotions occurs through spoken words. When children start school, they are normally able to self-regulate most emotional reactions, although they continue to need some help. This may be provided by parents, teachers, or members of their peer group.

Peer group
A group of people of about the same age and interests.

The infant bond

Most developmental psychologists believe that to survive and develop normally, all children must form an enduring emotional bond with a parent or caregiver early in infancy. The concept of bonding between infants and their mothers was one that psychologists borrowed from ethology. Konrad Lorenz (1903–1989) had a major effect on developmental psychology through his research into the nature of imprinting (bonding) in animals. One of his studies examined the behavior of goslings. Like many other birds, geese form an intense bond with the first thing that they see moving when they are newly hatched. Most often that

Ethology
The science of observing the natural behavior of different species of animals, including humans, in their own environments.

Harlow's Studies of Infant Monkeys

Sigmund Freud believed that mother and infant formed a very close emotional bond during the latter's first year of life. He proposed that this bond was a result of what he termed drive reduction—that is, infants must satisfy their need for nourishment, and mothers meet this need, thereby creating a strong emotional link with their infants.

Harry Harlow, a researcher who studied human development by conducting research on monkeys, was the first to test this theory. In the 1950s he conducted a series of experiments with newborn Rhesus monkeys raised without their mothers. Some of the infant monkeys were placed in cages where they had access to a wire model of a mother and a soft cloth model of a mother. In some conditions the infants were fed by the wire mother, and in others they were fed by the soft-cloth mother. The results of these experiments were very clear. The infant monkeys would spend virtually no time at all with the wire mother even when it was this model that fed them. Instead, they showed a strong preference for the soft-cloth mother, particularly when they became frightened. Harlow concluded that it was contact comfort, and not feeding, that promoted the formation of an attachment relationship between an infant and its mother.

Konrad Lorenz (right) combined an interest in zoology with his studies in psychology. This exploration of animal behavior led to the creation of modern ethology, or the comparative study of behavior in people and other animals. In 1973 Lorenz shared a Nobel Prize with Niko Tinbergen (left) and Karl von Frisch.

is the mother goose. This bond is essential to the goslings' survival because in order to avoid being eaten by predators, they must stay very close to the mother so that she can protect them.

Lorenz discovered that newly hatched goslings would even imprint on him if he was the first thing they saw moving; they would follow him around as though he was their mother. This innate, or inborn, ability to bond becomes less prominent and effective as time passes, suggesting that there is a critical or sensitive period in the development of geese for this imprinting to occur.

Attachment theory

At about the same time as Lorenz was conducting his research, John Bowlby (1907–1990) began formulating attachment theory. He believed that the bonding that occurs between infants and parents was too complex to be explained as a simple imprinting process. Bowlby observed many infants and young children who had been separated from either both of their parents or orphaned. He noticed that many such children seemed to suffer from the lack of a close intimate relationship with a parent or some other adult caregiver. He therefore proposed that there is an innate attachment system that links the infant to the mother.

Curriculum Context

Students may like to analyze Lorenz's work on imprinting and discuss how relevant it is when exploring human infant attachment.

This attachment system is driven by infants' need for security. When frightened, infants cry or, if able, crawl or walk toward their mother; ideally the mother responds sensitively by soothing and calming them. Once infants are calm again, they can carry on exploring their surroundings, knowing that the mother will be there to provide protection and safety. According to Bowlby, a healthy attachment relationship requires mothers to strike a balance between allowing infants to explore the world and making infants feel safe and secure without being overly protective.

Bowlby believed that these experiences with mothers and other caregivers became part of an internal working model of relationships, a schema or "road map" that represents for the infant the trustworthiness of other people. He also theorized that attachment in infancy will affect the quality of the children's social relationships with other people and also how they develop both socially and emotionally.

Schema
A model or outline of a theory.

Infant attachment

Mary Ainsworth (1913–1999) believed that it was important to consider why some infants and mothers developed a secure attachment relationship, while others did not. To understand this, she conducted a study in which she used extensive and detailed observations of mothers and older infants at home.

Ainsworth noticed that while some of the mothers responded immediately and sensitively to their infants' crying and distress, other mothers would not do so— some ignored their children altogether. Convinced that these differences were important, Ainsworth developed a laboratory procedure known as the Strange Situation that set out to measure children's attachment relationships: infants' reactions to separations and reunions with their mothers.

Bowlby's Development Stages

There has been a lot of research into the nature of the relationships between babies and the people who care for them. According to the British psychologist John Bowlby, the attachment relationship between parent and child is not inborn and does not emerge suddenly: It develops gradually over the first two years of life.

Bowlby described these changes as a series of stages in the first two years of life.

Stage 1: *Preattachment (0–2 months)*
Infants show no obvious preferences for caregivers and do not discriminate with whom they will interact.

Stage 2: *Attachment in the making (2–7 months)*
Infants begin showing clear signs of recognizing caregivers and siblings.

Stage 3: *Clear-cut attachment (7–24 months)*
At this stage children become distressed when they are separated from the mother or father and will be wary or show obvious signs of distress when around strangers. It is at this time that toddlers become skilled at communicating with caregivers and others in order to regain closeness and that feeling of security.

Stage 4: *Goal-corrected partnership (24 months onward)*
The relationship between children and caregivers becomes more balanced as children become aware of parent intentions and are capable of the verbal communication of needs.

Ainsworth's research highlighted four types of infant attachment relationships. Secure infants behave as though they are able to trust and rely on their caregivers when they are distressed. These secure infants become very upset when the parent leaves the room and are comforted quickly when she returns. Anxious ambivalent or resistant insecure infants show clear signs of distress when the parent leaves but cannot be comforted when their parents return. Anxious avoidant insecure infants often show few or no visible signs of distress when their parents leave or return; even if they do become upset when their parents leave, they seem to ignore the parents on their return. Finally, disorganized infants may seem secure and insecure at different points in separation and reunion with their parents, and sometimes show bizarre behaviors such as suddenly freezing, going into trances, or rocking back and forth continually.

Numerous studies have demonstrated that secure infants are most likely to develop normally in their social and emotional skills. They have more supportive relationships with friends and peers, and they are best able to cope with difficulties at home and in school. It is also clear that becoming a securely attached infant and child depends, in part, on parenting.

Attachment in adulthood

Attachment theorists have expanded this research to include attachment in adolescence and adulthood. They found that adults have internal working models of relationships based on their childhood relationships.

Secure, autonomous adults are those who have clear memories of their childhood experiences regardless of whether they are happy or unhappy memories. These secure adults have close relationships with friends and romantic partners and are able to get the social support they need. This category corresponds with the secure attachment classification found in infancy.

Dismissive adults are those who seem more autonomous and independent and minimize the importance of their relationships with parents and other people. This corresponds with the anxious avoidant attachment classification in infancy.

Enmeshed or preoccupied adults are anxious about their past and current relationships with their parents. They are sometimes so preoccupied by these concerns that it interferes with their ability to interact with others. This category corresponds with the anxious ambivalent or resistant insecure attachment classification in infancy.

Disorganized adults do not seem to have a structured attachment system. They have unclear memories of their pasts and are incapable of telling coherent stories about their relationships with parents and other

Adolescence

The period following the onset of puberty during which a child becomes an adult.

Autonomous

Acting independently.

Curriculum Context

Students should think about how relationships with caregivers in childhood might affect mental and emotional states in adulthood.

Research into attachment in adolescence and adulthood has shown that parenting and childrearing play a part in the way that teenagers interact with each other. Internal working models of relationships are based on relationships formed in childhood.

people. This category corresponds with the disorganized attachment classification in infancy.

Differences in parenting

In the mid-20th century, researchers began to realize that different forms of parenting behavior in a wide variety of cultures could be described by using two independent "dimensions" or attributes—parental warmth or acceptance and parental control or restriction of the child's behavior. One parent could be very warm and loving toward her children, but also highly restrictive, demanding that they behave according to her standards. In contrast, another parent might be warm and loving while exercising very little control. It became clear that, to describe and understand parenting and its effects on children, psychologists would need to consider the extent to which each parent was warm and controlling.

Baumrind's parenting styles

In the 1960s and 1970s Diana Baumrind (born 1927) proposed that these two dimensions of parenting behavior could be used to define several meaningful categories of parenting types or styles.

Authoritative parents are those who are relatively high in warmth and moderate to high in control of their children. They tend to be firm with their children and are certain to correct them for misbehaving. However, these parents also make it clear to their children that they are loved and accepted and they have a close and warm relationship with their children. Baumrind and others found that the children of authoritative parents are well adjusted, socially and emotionally mature, and competent. These children are most likely to do well in school and to have good relationships with their peers.

Authoritarian parents also exercise moderate to high levels of control but they are harsh, negative, and sometimes hostile toward their children. Baumrind discovered that these parents were less effective at promoting healthy social and emotional development in their children. Research suggests that children of authoritarian parents are more likely to be immature, socially incompetent, and negative in their emotions. They tend to underperform at school and have less successful relationships with others.

> **Authoritarian**
> Enforcing obedience to authority, at the expense of personal freedom.

Permissive parents exercise very little control over their children, typically ignoring misbehavior. At the same time, they are also warm and supportive. Baumrind believed children brought up in this way would lack the basic social skills needed to be competent in peer relationships and to do well in school.

> **Curriculum Context**
> Many curricula require students to debate whether sociocultural factors can reliably predict individual success.

Daycare and development

If attachment to caregivers is formed in infancy, what happens to infants who are placed in day care during

The social and emotional skills these children develop at kindergarten will depend in part on how their parents have treated them. Secure infants are comforted by their parents when they are distressed, and this lays the foundations for the development of supportive relationships with the children they meet when they are older.

the first or second year of life? Are these infants unable to form attachment relationships with their parents? Are their attachment relationships compromised or impaired by frequent separation from their mothers and fathers? Does being away from parents early in life lead to problems in social, emotional, or cognitive development?

Today most children in most industrial nations are in some form of nonparental childcare by the time they are three years old, and a significant minority of infants and toddlers are also placed in day care. This shift in childrearing patterns has arisen as a result of dramatic changes in women's career development and adult employment patterns.

Impact on attachment
In the 1980s researchers began studying the effect of infant day care on infant attachment and other

developmental outcomes, but the findings were not conclusive. Jay Belsky claimed these studies showed that infants who were placed in day care in the first year of life for more than 20 hours a week were more likely to have an insecure attachment relationship with their mothers. A more recent study suggests that, for most infants, being placed in day care does not present a risk to the attachment relationship with the parents: A sensitive and responsive mother is more important to the formation of a secure attachment relationship, regardless of whether the infant attends day care. Some research suggests that day care can even have a positive influence on children's cognitive development, particularly those in higher-risk home circumstances.

The New York Longitudinal Study

U.S. psychologists Alexander Thomas and Stella Chess conducted the New York Longitudinal Study, beginning in the 1950s, in which they examined temperament in a group of infants and followed them until they started school.

Chess and Thomas were able to identify nine attributes that were crucial for characterizing differences in infant and child temperament. They were: (1) activity level; (2) regularity of feeding, sleeping, and toilet schedule; (3) reactivity or response to the presentation of a new person (a stranger) or new object; (4) sensitivity to experiences in the environment; (5) adaptability, or the ability to adjust to sudden changes in the environment; (6) intensity of behaviors; (7) attention and the ability to persist with a task; (8) distractibility; and (9) overall mood (irritable, happy, sad, or withdrawn).

Thomas and Chess defined three groups of infants. The largest group, easy babies, are adaptive, well regulated, attentive, happy, and content, and not overly sensitive to changes in the environment, such as being moved to a new location or the removal of a toy. In contrast, difficult babies are far less adaptable. They are fussy and cry frequently, are difficult to soothe, and are not well regulated in their sleeping, eating, and toilet schedules. Their reactions to changes in the environment are intense and frequent. Finally, slow-to-warm-up babies were not happy and content like easy babies but were not intensely irritable like difficult babies. They showed low levels of energy and would often withdraw from new people or situations; and although they were often crying and fussy, these negative moods were generally mild. About one-third of the children in this study could not be classified because they did not show a clear pattern of behaviors and moods based on these nine attributes.

Social Development

People are distinct from all other animals in the complexity of their social behavior. Yet we come into the world with no understanding of others, lacking the basic communication skills required to interact. Early friendships are the key to having healthy social relationships throughout our lives.

Sibling

A brother or sister.

Theories about the development of the "self"—our identity and the concepts that we have about our interests and abilities—have been proposed by social scientists for more than a century. In 1902 Charles Horton Cooley (1864–1929) proposed that the "self" is a reflection of how others see us. If our parents, siblings, and peers tell us that we are clever, good looking, and athletic, then we are likely to perceive ourselves in these ways. If people treat us as dull and unattractive, then we are likely to see ourselves that way.

A sense of others

George Mead (1863–1931) thought that children's understanding of self and others develops simultaneously through social interactions. As children develop the skills that enable them to communicate with others, they acquire knowledge about themselves and learn how to see the world from other people's points of view. Young children use their knowledge of themselves and others in "pretend games" when they act out being both themselves and the parents.

Curriculum Context

Students may find it useful to compare their own memories of developing social awareness with those of their friends.

Intersubjectivity

The face-to-face eye contact between a caregiver and an infant is termed primary intersubjectivity and occurs from early in life. During these exchanges the infant learns important new skills about turn-taking.

Toward the end of the first year of life, secondary intersubjectivity appears. Infant and caregiver interact with each other as they did before, but they are now

In dressing up for Halloween, these children are playing with their emerging sense of self-identity and how others see them. As children grow up, they begin to define themselves in relation to their friends. It is not until adolescence and young adulthood that people become aware of the relationship between how we see ourselves and how other people see us.

able to include other things—objects, people, the family dog, or a loud noise—into their "conversation." As infants get older, they become better at pointing out objects and other people, and this expands these interactions. Throughout the development of these skills, infants are learning about the social rules of communication and about their ability to interact with the world and other individuals.

The "still face" paradigm

Infants develop expectations about other people's social behavior from a surprisingly young age. This discovery was made using an experimental procedure called the still face. The researcher places an infant in a baby seat and asks someone to sit in front of the infant. The adult engages the infant in face-to-face interaction by making eye contact, talking, and cooing. The infant responds by making eye contact, smiling, and making sounds and facial expressions. After a few minutes the adult freezes her face into a neutral expression. Infants do not like this. Many show signs of frustration or anger; other infants seem fearful or sad. They know that a rule of normal social behavior has been broken.

Paradigm
A typical example of something; a model.

During the first six to eight weeks, infants smile using just the lower portions of the face. These smiles can be triggered by the infants' physical state or by stroking their cheeks. From two to three months of age, infants begin responding with true social smiling—a voluntary smile that involves the entire face. People are able to make infants smile by speaking to them, making close face contact, or by showing them something amusing.

Social referencing occurs when an infant looks to the face of a caregiver to gain information about how she or he should be feeling. For example, if a stranger appears, the infant is uncertain and feels frightened. He looks at his father's face. Because he is smiling and reassuring, the baby understands that he need not be afraid.

Self-concept

Psychologists use the term "self-concept" to describe the set of ideas that individuals hold about themselves. Children's self-concepts change as they gain new experiences and as their brains develop and provide them with more skills for thinking and problem solving.

Curriculum Context

Students should be able to identify typical changes in self-concept from early childhood to adolescence.

H. Rudolph Schaffer (born 1926) suggests that the changes can be described in five ways. First, the self-concept changes from being very simple to being highly complex. While young children describe themselves using the most general terms, older children and adolescents give longer and more precise descriptions that take many factors into account. Second, young children are notoriously unreliable in their self-descriptions. As children get older, they become more consistent.

Third, self-concepts change from being focused on concrete terms to emphasizing abstract ideas. For example, young children are more likely to talk and think about themselves in terms of what they look like and what they are good at. As they get older, their self-understanding and descriptions turn toward internal states or feelings and the functioning of the mind.

Fourth, self-concepts increasingly emphasize comparisons with others. As they develop, children compare themselves to other children. This shift can be a problem because of its potentially negative effect on developing self-esteem.

Fifth, there is an important change in the public versus private nature of the self. Children do not begin thinking about the privacy of the self-concept until late in middle childhood. Adolescents spend much time pondering their private sense of identity, a change that is accompanied by greater self-consciousness and concern about how others see them.

Young Children's Self-Concepts

One way to get young children to provide information about their self-concepts is to engage them in puppet play, using two puppets that describe different types of children. One puppet represents a child who likes to watch lightning during a storm, while the other puppet represents a child who does not like watching lightning and hides during a storm. After watching the puppets act out their roles, the children choose the puppet they are most like. More reliable reports can be gathered if the children are not forced to make a choice between the puppets. Instead of asking the children to choose which puppet they are most like, the researcher asks, "What are you like?"

Understanding others

Researchers have identified five stages of development in children's understanding of others. During the first stage (from about three to five years of age), children do not understand that other people's views may be different from their own. During the second stage (about five to eight years of age) children come to recognize that people often have different perspectives, but they are not yet able to integrate these different perspectives into their understanding of self versus other. During the third stage (about eight years of age to the end of childhood), children begin to think about their own and others' viewpoints; they are now able to be introspective about possible differences between themselves and others. However, they cannot hold these multiple perspectives in mind at the same time. That skill is acquired in the fourth stage, early adolescence. During the fifth and final stage (from midadolescence to adulthood), teenagers develop the skills to compare many perspectives to many others. They can understand the viewpoints of abstract groups, such as society at large or an ethnic group.

Self-esteem

An important part of our self-concept is our self-esteem. Self-esteem emerges as we develop an understanding of our own strengths and weaknesses compared to those of others. Self-esteem varies widely between individuals and our feelings about our own worthiness and competence can change dramatically.

In the 1980s Susan Harter devised tests that measure children's self-esteem. In these tests, children describe whether they are more or less athletic than others, better or worse at school, more or less attractive, and so on. Also, they describe the extent to which these abilities or attributes are or are not important to them. Low self-esteem arises when children have low self-worth regarding abilities that truly matter to them. A child may have high self-esteem in some domains but low self-esteem in others. Children and adults who have high self-esteem most of the time tend to be more ambitious and more successful. Individuals with low self-esteem are more likely to suffer from anxiety and to withdraw from social interactions.

Curriculum Context

Students might consider how low self-esteem adversely affects social interactions.

Identity exploration and commitment

The final outcome of the developing sense of self is the formation of a stable personal identity. Erik

During adolescence we develop a sense of identity—who we are and what we are going to do in life. This can be a difficult and challenging time as individuals analyze their own past and future, and also challenge the beliefs and behavior of family members and their peer group.

Erikson (1902–1994) proposed that adolescence is the crucial period in the development of identity formation. It is during adolescence that we understand who we are and where we are going. In the 1960s James Marcia tested some of the ideas in Erikson's theory. From interviews with young adults, Marcia identified two aspects of identity formation: identity exploration and identity commitment.

Identity exploration occurs when adolescents investigate their own beliefs, plans for the future, and understanding of the past. It involves thinking about family members, peers, and friends, and who they are as individuals. Some adolescents consider these matters carefully and are able to describe their exploration, while others do not consider them at all.

Identity commitment is the degree to which the adolescent or young adult holds a firm belief in her own attitudes and aspirations. While some adolescents have a strong desire to realize their goals, others take few steps toward fulfilling their plans.

Curriculum Context

Students may be asked to explain the stages involved in Erikson's developmental model.

Four identity statuses

Marcia also identified four patterns, called statuses, in adolescents' search for an identity. Identity diffusion is the status of adolescents and young adults who do not actively explore their personal identities and who lack clear goals and commitments. Identity moratorium occurs among individuals who are in the midst of deep exploration but have not yet committed to a particular identity. Identity foreclosure occurs when an individual commits to an identity before he or she has examined carefully his or her own beliefs, experiences, and goals. Identity achievement occurs among those individuals who have thoroughly examined their beliefs and aspirations and have formed a strong commitment to their emerging identity.

Gender

Another important component of the self-concept is the understanding of one's own gender. Gender refers to the behavior, attitudes, and goals society considers appropriate for males and females.

Curriculum Context

Many curricula expect students to explain how gender identity develops.

From an early age, boys and girls begin to show differences in their toy preferences. Boys are more likely to be attracted by vehicles and similar objects, while girls are more likely to play with dolls. From about two years old throughout childhood and into adulthood, males show more aggression than females. Girls can be aggressive, too, but boys are more likely to show physical or verbal aggression, while girls are more likely to be aggressive using subtler means, such as excluding children from play or by spreading rumors.

From about three years of age until midadolescence, children have a strong preference for playing with same-sex peers. Girls' groups of friends are smaller and more exclusive than boys' groups. Boys play in larger, more inclusive groups. The fact that it is very difficult to get children to behave otherwise suggests that this behavior is biologically determined.

Gender concepts

In the first several years of life, children acquire the labels for "boy" and "girl" and learn to apply these labels to themselves and to others. Children of this age rely heavily on obvious physical features to distinguish between men and women. From around the age of six or seven, children acquire an adult-like understanding of gender. They now understand that gender and physical appearance can be distinct; for example, a man can have long hair or a woman can wear trousers.

For decades, developmental psychologists have debated how children's concepts of gender influence their behavior. On one hand, gender differences are seen as genetic (inherited); according to the other theory they are socialized (learned). These two approaches have been integrated in what is called the gender schema theory, which suggests that children's understanding of gender is filtered through their existing ideas of how girls and boys look and behave.

Curriculum Context

Students should explore the issue of how gender discrimination affects development.

False Appearances

In studies carried out in the 1970s and 1980s, B. Lloyd and C. Smith asked women who were themselves mothers to look after six-month-old babies whom they had not met before. Some of the boys were presented as girls, girls as boys. Regardless of the children's biological sex, the women treated them in a way that was consistent with their apparent gender. When a woman played with a baby named and dressed as a boy, she usually offered it a masculine toy, such as a rubber hammer. If she thought it was a girl, she gave it soft, furry toys. The women also responded differently to how the babies played. If a child named and dressed as a boy played in a physically robust way, the women joined in and encouraged the child. If a "girl" behaved in the same way, the women saw this as a sign of distress and talked soothingly to the child.

A female architect at work. Traditionally architecture has been viewed as a male profession, but women are now enjoying careers in this field. Notions about acceptable careers or hobbies for men and for women have changed throughout the centuries and also vary between cultures.

Newborn babies enter the world color-coded according to gender: blue for boys, pink for girls. Long before sex differences in behavior appear, parents and others behave differently toward girls and boys. Mothers spend more time talking with infant daughters than they do with infant sons. Men are more likely than women to play with their children in a physically engaging, rough-and-tumble way, particularly if it is play with a son. Parents also prefer their children to play with gender-appropriate toys. In conversations with their daughters, mothers use more terms that describe emotions than they do with their sons. Parents will often tolerate aggression in a son.

Ethnic identity

From preschool years, children show an awareness of their own and others' ethnicity. At this age they rely on physical features such as skin tone and facial features to define ethnic groups. By middle childhood, children are aware of their own ethnicities, and they tend to use more subtle aspects of cultural practices and attitudes to define ethnic groups.

Before adolescence children do not closely examine their ethnic identity. Exploration of ethnic identity

Ethnicity

The state of belonging to a group of people who share a common race or culture.

occurs when young teenagers become more aware of differences in cultural practices and behaviors, and when they learn about the social, political, and economic injustices that often exist for ethnic minorities. During this stage of development the adolescent no longer takes for granted the attitudes and behaviors of the majority ethnic group. In the final stage, at the end of adolescence, young adults achieve a coherent ethnic identity.

Understanding morality

In 1932 Jean Piaget proposed that morality develops in stages and that moral development goes hand in hand with children's ability to reason. He described three stages of moral reasoning that all children move through. During stage one (birth to four years of age), children lack even the most basic abilities to ponder questions of morality. Although young children are capable of learning basic social rules, they exercise them as a result of social learning.

During stage two (four to nine years), children acquire a naive understanding of why we have rules and codes of conduct. They believe that the rules cannot be changed. Adults enforce the rules, and children comply in deference to their unquestioned authority.

It is during the third and final stage (nine years of age and later) that children develop the ability to evaluate their own and others' behaviors. They become aware that the rules of moral conduct are a part of our culture, and that they can and do change. Children begin to understand that we comply with the rules of morality because we choose to adhere to a high principle or standard.

Levels of morality

Lawrence Kohlberg (1927–1987) identified a total of six stages that span three levels of moral reasoning.

The first level of moral reasoning, which Kohlberg called preconventional morality, has two stages. During stage one (before seven or eight years of age), children determine right and wrong based on rules and punishment. They make decisions about how to behave based on avoiding punishment. In stage two (eight to ten years of age), children come to see morality as simple justice based on equal treatment of self and other and they understand that other people's needs and wants are important.

Curriculum Context

Many curricula expect students to list the stages in the development of morality.

Level two, conventional morality, includes two stages. During stage three (10 or 11 years of age and later), the emphasis shifts toward doing what pleases and helps others. There is a comparable transition toward considering our own and others' intentions and motives, and this internal motivation becomes the driving force behind moral behavior. During stage four—adolescence and young adulthood—individuals emphasize the importance of the society's standards of behavior. Being good means obeying authority and respecting the social order in order to avoid chaos.

Level three, postconventional morality, includes two more stages and is acquired in adulthood by a small

Kohlberg's Moral Dilemmas: The Heinz Story

In order to assess moral development, Kohlberg used short stories that presented the individual with a moral dilemma that he or she was then asked to solve. The classic dilemma involves a man named Heinz who has a dear wife who is very ill. Without a particular medication Heinz's wife will die. A pharmacist has the necessary drug, but he charges a very high price for it and refuses to sell it to Heinz at a price he can afford.

In desperation Heinz steals the drug so that his wife can live, even though he realizes that by doing so he is breaking the law.

Should Heinz have stolen the drug? Why or why not? What else could he have done? What would you do if you were in this situation, and why? According to Kohlberg, only people who reach the final stage of moral development break the law for universal moral principles.

minority of individuals. During stage five, individuals gain an understanding that laws and social rules are framed by fallible people, are not necessarily fair in all circumstances, and can be changed or challenged. During stage six, the individual follows universal moral principles—codes of conduct that override the majority view about appropriate behavior.

The role of friendship

Children's friendships play a crucial role in social development. Researchers have addressed questions about the formation of and changes in friendships, how children form and change their social standing in the larger peer group, and how these relationships affect children's mental health and development.

When stable friendships first emerge in children's lives, the emphasis is on proximity and being friendly. Typical five- or six-year-olds will say that another child is their friend because they are in the same class, and because they are friendly and share toys. Most children show frequent changes in who they are friends with.

In middle childhood, children are more likely to define their friendships in terms of loyalty and trust as well as shared attributes or desires. In the transition to adolescence, children come to understand friendships as being opportunities for intimacy and emotional support. Adolescents and adults describe their friendships in terms of closeness, affection, and trust.

John Gottman devised an experiment to study the formation of friendships in childhood. He took children of the same age who did not know each other and randomly paired them. The children met for several play sessions for a month, and their interactions were videotaped. Gottman identified several factors that accounted for which children became friends. Future friends were children who

Fallible
Capable of making mistakes.

Curriculum Context

Students might find it useful to consider and discuss with each other how their own personal friendships changed from early childhood to adolescence.

Friendships play a crucial role in social development. The nature of friendship changes as the person matures. Young children play together and share toys, whereas teenagers rely on friends for emotional support.

were likely to discuss and agree on a shared activity that they both enjoyed. They were also more likely to disclose and exchange information. Their personal disclosures served to show that they trusted each other. Friends-to-be were also clearer in their communication with each other, which reduced the risk of conflict between them.

Gottman's research showed that friendships are a training ground for conflict resolution. Stable and supportive friendships develop between partners who are able to sort out their disagreements and learn how to avoid future conflicts. Highly aggressive children find it difficult to form lasting friendships.

Status in the group

Researchers study and evaluate children's status in their peer groups. Each child in a group is interviewed separately. During the interview the child is given a list of all the children in that group and is asked questions such as: (1) Who are your closest friends? (2) Name the children that you like the most. (3) Name the children that you like the least. (4) Name the children who start fights a lot. From the answers, the investigator gets an idea of who is liked or disliked, and who children think is well-behaved or badly behaved.

Popular children are those named by many other children as being well-liked. Rejected children are those who are named by many other children as being disliked. Neglected children are those who are not named at all. Average or typical children are those who are mentioned by some of their peers as being well-liked, but mentioned by others as being disliked. Each child's status in the peer group can remain the same or change over a period of time, although many rejected children tend to remain in the rejected group.

Curriculum Context

It may be useful to identify the important factors that help or hinder friendships.

Adolescent friendships

As children move into adolescence, they spend less and less time with their parents and siblings and more and more time with their friends. They begin to take on the values, attitudes, and styles of behavior of their friends. Although children tend to be like their friends in terms of personality, academic achievement, and attitudes, it is not clear how friendship similarity arises. Is it because children choose friends who are most like themselves (selection) or is it because children who spend a lot of time together teach each other how to behave and what to believe (socialization)?

Research has shown how selection and socialization influence friendships among antisocial and delinquent youths. Aggressive children are likely to be rejected by their peers. By the time they are young adolescents, they are likely to have only a few friendships, which tend to be with similarly antisocial youths. Antisocial adolescents teach each other how to become even more antisocial. They reinforce each other's antisocial attitudes by showing approval for delinquent acts. They also teach each other new antisocial behaviors. Antisocial acts and attitudes become the social "glue" for delinquent teenagers' relationships. When antisocial adolescents and young adults form romantic attachments, partners tend to be alike in prior and current antisocial behaviors.

Delinquent

Having a tendency to commit crime.

Applications and Future Challenges

Psychological study of human development from fetus to adulthood is a rapidly changing field. Psychologists have utilized technological advances such as genetic profiling, which are expected to bring about improved treatments of mental illnesses.

Genetics

The properties or features of an organism that are inherited from previous generations.

During the last 100 years, psychologists have radically altered the way they view subjects such as childhood development, the nature and importance of families, and mental disorder. Research into genetics, the development of the brain, and the significance of national and cultural influences have embedded within psychology a range of scientific principles.

Studying brain development

For many years, scientific opinion was divided over whether human personality and development were dependent on biological causes (nature) or on the external influence of circumstance and the environment (nurture). Psychologists now recognize that people develop through constant interaction between the two. Research in several disciplines has helped them reach this conclusion, notably genetics and cognitive neuroscience.

Cognitive neuroscience

The study of the brain and its processes.

The last quarter of the 20th century saw a dramatic increase in the quantity and quality of research into brain development in infancy and early childhood. Scientists gained important new insights into how early experiences may influence subsequent cognitive and social-emotional development through their effects on the brain.

Meanwhile, there remains some debate among neuroscientists and psychologists about whether the early years really are the most important in brain development. Some researchers think that the brain is an organ that can adapt to change throughout life, regardless of experiences in infancy and childhood. Nor is it clear how much the development of the brain depends on external environmental cues, or how lasting the effects of influences such as malnutrition and poverty are on the brains of young children. Despite these uncertainties, modern psychologists know a great deal about the way the brain grows and functions in early childhood, and how the functions of the nervous system influence thought, the emotions, and behavior. This knowledge helps them advise on child development with increasing conviction.

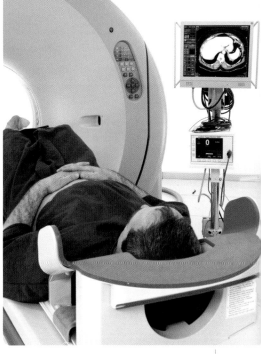

It is now known that when we are born, the brain is not intact; it continues to develop rapidly—often in spurts—throughout childhood and adolescence. Evidence from studies of animals suggests the brain reorganizes as a result of changes in the levels of hormones (messenger chemicals) during puberty.

Second, scientists have shown that brain growth partly depends on exposure to particular stimuli. For some parts of the brain these stimuli must be received at a precise stage of development, while for other parts the stimuli may be effective regardless of the stage at which they occur. By studying the timing and nature of the stimuli, it is possible that psychologists will soon be able to determine the treatments needed to reverse the effects of some neurological disorders.

This patient has just undergone an MRI scan. The MRI scanner contains a powerful magnet that causes different chemicals within the brain to emit distinctive radio signals. Using these signals, a series of 2-D slices through the brain can be shown.

Third, it has been discovered that even though the brain develops most rapidly early in life, it is capable of change throughout its existence. For example older adults who consistently use their brains to solve problems, play computer games, or work creatively are more likely to retain the use of neural systems that may otherwise deteriorate if the brain is not actively engaged. Brain power may need regular exercise to stay in shape. By further investigating these changes in brain development throughout the human life span, psychologists hope to find treatments that will reduce the deterioration in mental function that is normally associated with senility.

The genetics of psychology
Scientists are also making discoveries about the influence of genetics on a range of psychological attributes. These include intelligence, personality, emotions, and mental illnesses and disorders.

Psychologists have long considered the contribution of genetic factors to human social and emotional development. Years of behavioral studies using identical and nonidentical twins, full and half siblings, and adoptive and step-siblings have shown that genetic heritage can have a major influence on many psychological attributes, including personality traits.

Although the importance of genetic influences is now universally recognized, how they operate to produce psychological characteristics such as personality and emotions is poorly understood. However, there have been recent advances in scientific techniques for acquiring and analyzing human deoxyribonucleic acid (DNA). DNA is the molecule that forms the basis of the genetic code

These girls are identical twins. Researchers have used both identical and nonidentical twins extensively to try to shed more light on the "nature versus nurture" debate about personality, cognitive development, and psychological disorder.

that people inherit from their parents. Scientists can now investigate human DNA for the genetic signatures of a variety of traits, including intelligence, schizophrenia, aggression, and dementia.

Most of the psychological research programs emerging from this genetic revolution are concerned with making improvements in diagnosis and new types of treatments. Examples include prenatal tests for Down syndrome, fragile-X syndrome, and phenylketonuria. These disorders account for many cases of mental retardation. Several genetic markers for Alzheimer's disease have also been identified. In addition, genetic signatures have been identified as possible causes of attention deficit hyperactivity disorder (ADHD).

Recent scientific breakthroughs are leading many psychologists to reflect on the ethics of genetic treatments and research. For how long, and in what ways, should we store and protect the genetic material of research volunteers? Is it right or wrong to alter people's DNA in order to change their lives according to a psychological preconception of normality? These and many other ethical questions remain the subjects of intense scrutiny and debate.

Adapting to changing times
Psychologists increasingly recognize the importance of studying the rearing environments or "contexts" of child development. The study of changes in contexts has provided them with a mass of information about the ways we adapt to our surroundings.

One of the most astounding contextual changes over the last century has been the improvements in medical technology that have enabled many more "high-risk" infants to survive than ever before. This includes infants that are born prematurely and well below a healthy birthweight. In many nations it is now common for

Schizophrenia
A long-term mental disorder characterized by abnormalities in the perception or expression of reality.

Alzheimer's disease
An incurable disease that causes loss of memory and other cognitive skills in later life.

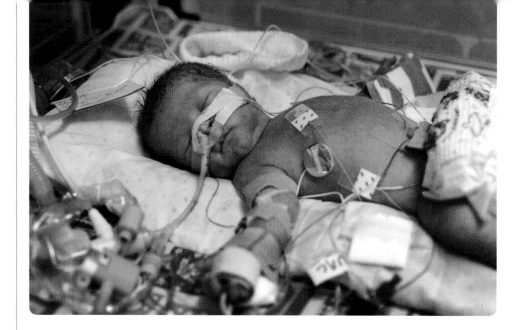

With increasing numbers of premature babies surviving each year, psychologists are studying the longer-term effects of premature birth on psychological health.

Gestation

The time spent in the womb between conception and birth.

Neonatal

Relating to newborn children.

babies who are born before 27 weeks gestation or that weigh less than 2 pounds (0.9 kg) to survive and grow to adulthood. This is due largely to the widespread establishment of neonatal intensive care units (NICUs). These institutions have equipment and trained staff who are able to keep premature babies alive long enough for their bodies and brains to "catch up" in developmental terms. Doctors now understand that these high-risk infants should not be isolated, but instead must have frequent physical contact with parents and caregivers for them to develop normally.

Longer-term studies of high-risk infants have demonstrated that some parenting factors are critical for the subsequent health and development of a child. Once an infant is well enough to leave hospital, the mother's health and behavior toward that infant become extremely important. Mothers who are sensitive and responsive to the needs of their children maximize the chances of the infants showing normal emotional, social, and cognitive development.

However, even the most sensitive and nurturing caregiving will not create a child who is psychologically healthy if profound damage has occurred to the central nervous system or other key organs within the infant's body. Babies of low birthweight may face many years of health and developmental problems, causing intense strain for parents and family members alike. As more of these infants survive, higher numbers of families will need increased support from medical and psychological professionals.

The Roots of Resilience

Many of the world's children and adolescents live without adequate shelter, food, water, or healthcare. Researchers have long been interested in the roots of resilience—the ability that some of these high-risk children have not only to survive but to thrive. Psychologists hope that the identification of these resiliency factors will lead to new treatments that will dramatically improve the mental health of many high-risk children.

Emmy Werner and Ruth Smith studied an entire group of infants born on the Hawaiian island of Kauai in 1955. They followed the children and their families through infancy, adolescence, and into adulthood, and conducted many assessments of a wide range of outcomes.

Of nearly 700 children who were first included in the study, about one-third were at risk of developmental problems. The risks were caused by factors including birth complications, such as premature birth and low birthweight, poverty, and mentally ill parents. Despite these factors, the researchers found that many of these high-risk children developed into healthy, happy adults.

Werner and Smith discovered factors that explained why these infants were thriving. They included having a close sibling relationship, good attention from caregivers in early childhood, strong family ties in the immediate and extended family, and few stressful life events, such as the death of a parent, divorce, or other upheavals.

The human-computer interface

Another dramatic social change of the last 30 years has been the increase in the use of computers and computer games by children and adolescents. What are the long-term psychological consequences of computer and computer game use? Are there benefits for the social, emotional, and cognitive development of children? If so, are there also costs? What specific

This girl is chatting with a friend on the Internet. The long-term social and developmental effects of spending hours each day online are the focus of a great deal of research.

aspects of these new technologies promote optimal development?

Computer games tend to be more widely used by boys than by girls. Many of these games require fast thinking, strategy-building, attention, and visual-spatial skills. There is some evidence that playing games that require the use of perceptual and cognitive faculties may help strengthen these skills.

There is also growing interest in the effects of computer use on children's social lives. Computers and computer games have the potential to create problems for children who are already in danger of becoming socially isolated, while the same technologies may provide benefits to children who are not at risk.

There is mounting concern about the use of computer video games that depict violence. Studies have shown that some of the more violent games can promote aggression in children. Just how the use of these and other video games influences the development of social behavior remains an important question, which future research on computer use and child development will need to address.

Cultural differences

While studying adaptations to a changing world, psychologists have also begun to study differences in human development between different cultures. The study of cultural influences may lead to discoveries about specific environmental factors that contribute to psychological development. Psychologists can compare and contrast two different cultural groups in which a particular child-rearing practice is common in one but rare or absent in the other. That enables them to determine the possible effects of particular child-rearing practices on the social, emotional, and cognitive development of children.

Studies of child-rearing practices in different cultural groups have revealed remarkable variations in the experiences of children and adolescents. Research into parenting in nations such as the United Kingdom and the United States has focused on two-parent families, and especially on the relative contributions of each parent to the care of the child. Compared to most mothers, most fathers are less involved in the day-to-day care of their children. The mother tends to be the preferred parent when a child needs to be comforted. Some of the variations can be ascribed to biological differences between men and women.

Curriculum Context

Students should try to imagine how specific cultural differences in child-rearing might affect children's social development.

However, the conclusion that these differences are due solely to biology has been challenged by cross-cultural research. Recently, psychologists have studied naturally occurring variations in the ways that men and women divide child-rearing tasks in different contexts, ranging from gay- and lesbian-parent households in North America to polygamous communities in Africa. These studies have revealed some surprising information about family structure, gender, and parenting behaviors. Though much remains to be learned, these studies suggest that although family structures adapt to economic, social, and political forces, a child's need for nurturing and attentive caregiving exists in all cultural settings. Both men and women—whether biological parents or not—are capable of meeting this need.

Polygamous

Relating to one person with several marriage partners.

For example, anthropologists have conducted much research on the family structure of the Aka people of Central Africa. In this hunter-gatherer culture, fathers

Anthropologists

Scientists who study human zoology, evolution, and culture.

spend much more time holding their infants and toddlers than they do in other cultures. Aka mothers and fathers alike spend most of their playtime with their infants in face-to-face social interaction. Aka fathers are more likely to soothe and calm, clean, and show love and affection for their children than are the mothers. The bulk of the mothers' physical contact with their children involves feeding and carrying them. These behaviors challenge our western stereotypes of the separate nature of "fathering" and "mothering."

Lesbian and Gay Parents

Over the last decade psychologists researching cultural variations in child-rearing practice have broadened their studies to include the development and psychological health of children raised in households with two mothers or two fathers. Are children with lesbian or gay parents psychologically different when compared to the children of heterosexual parents?

There have been relatively few studies to date, and none at all have examined the long-term effects of such family structures. However, the data so far suggest that most of these children do not stand a significantly higher risk of developing social and emotional problems as long as they are part of a stable household.

As with other family structures, healthy psychological development of children living in single-sex households appears to depend on the provision of love, attention, and the opportunities for learning that the children need.

Investigating group childcare

For decades, the prevailing view has been that an infant's psychological development may be compromised by frequent, prolonged separations from the mother. At the same time, we have witnessed dramatic changes in social attitudes about the use of group care for infants and preschool children. It is now common for young children to be placed in family day care (small facilities that operate from the proprietor's own home) or day-care centers (large, specialized childcare facilities). Some psychologists have suggested that this shift in childcare practice has placed the mental health of whole generations of children in jeopardy, while others have maintained that this risk has been exaggerated. An intensive research effort is now under way, and comparisons between different cultural groups have been particularly useful in informing this debate.

One example of group childcare emerged after 1948 in the kibbutzim of Israel. On a kibbutz the whole community shares the provision of services, food, and shelter, and there is a strong emphasis on an equal distribution of wealth. From early in their lives, children living on a kibbutz spend lots of time during the day in groups with a caregiver. Shared caregiving for children is a way of life that is consistent with the kibbutzim philosophy, with its emphasis on equality and egalitarianism.

The long-standing presence of group childcare in Israeli kibbutzim, along with the rapid increases in group childcare in other nations such as the United States, has led psychologists to study how these contexts influence the psychological development of children. Researchers have found that children living on a kibbutz do not stand a higher risk of relationship problems with their parents than other Israeli children. Nor does the kibbutz lifestyle put them at a higher risk of behavioral or emotional problems. Similarly, studies of the effects of group childcare on child development in North America and Europe suggest that group care of sufficiently good quality does not negatively affect development. Research suggests that the quality of care matters more than the social setting, or the relationship of the child to the caregiver.

However, other research projects have shown that millions of children around the world are exposed to inadequate childcare in group settings. Solving this conundrum is one of the biggest challenges faced by developmental psychologists in the 21st century.

Kibbutz
(plural kibbutzim) A farm or factory in which all wealth is held in common, and all the children living there are raised collectively.

Egalitarianism
The belief that all people deserve equal rights and opportunities.

Conundrum
A difficult problem.

Glossary

Abstract Existing as an idea but having no physical existence.

Adolescence The period following the onset of puberty during which a child becomes an adult.

Alzheimer's disease An incurable disease that causes loss of memory and other cognitive skills in later life.

Amniotic sac The fluid-filled membrane that encloses the fetus.

Analogically Using knowledge about past situations to deal with new ones.

Anthropologists Scientists who study human zoology, evolution, and culture.

Articulated Formed clearly and distinctly.

Authoritarian Enforcing obedience to authority, at the expense of personal freedom.

Autonomous Acting independently.

Behaviorist Relating to the theory that behavior can be explained by conditioning alone.

Central nervous system The brain and the spinal cord.

Cerebral cortex The outer layer of the brain that plays an important part in consciousness.

Chronology The arrangement of events in the order in which they occur.

Cognitive Relating to the gaining of knowledge and understanding through thought, experience, and the senses.

Cognitive functions Those behaviors that are driven from the cortex of the brain and are also high-level processing, such as memory recall, language, or reasoning.

Cognitive neuroscience The study of the brain and its processes.

Compliant Inclined to obey rules or agree with others.

Conceptual Based on mental concepts, or ideas.

Concrete Existing in a physical form.

Constraints Limitations or restrictions.

Conundrum A difficult problem.

Delinquent Having a tendency to commit crime.

Egalitarianism The belief that all people deserve equal rights and opportunities.

Egocentric Thinking only of oneself without regard for the feelings of others.

Electrode The conductor through which electricity enters or leaves an object.

Embryo An unborn human baby in the eight weeks after conception. After eight weeks it is called a fetus.

Equilibrium The state in which opposing forces are balanced.

Ethnicity The state of belonging to a group of people who share a common race or culture.

Ethology The science of observing the natural behavior of different species of animals, including humans, in their own environments.

Fallible Capable of making mistakes.

Generic Relating to a group of things.

Genetics The properties or features of an organism that are inherited from previous generations.

Gestation The time spent in the womb between conception and birth.

Habituation The process of becoming familiar and disinterested.

Hierarchy A system in which things or groups of things are ranked one above another according to status.

Internalize To incorporate something within the self, either consciously or subconsciously, as a guiding principle.

Introspective Concerning the examination of one's own thoughts and emotions.

Kibbutz (plural kibbutzim) A farm or factory in which all wealth is held in common, and all the children living there are raised collectively.

Mental representation An image or idea that is stored in the memory and can be accessed at will.

Metacognitive Concerning awareness of one's own thought processes.

Modular Self-contained and separate from each other.

Morality Principles concerning right and wrong or good and bad behavior.

Neonatal Relating to newborn children.

Neurons Brain cells specialized to conduct nerve impulses.

Occipital cortex Part of the cerebral cortex concerned with visual processing.

Orientation The relative position or direction of something.

Paradigm A typical example of something; a model.

Parietal cortex Part of the cerebral cortex concerned with integrating sensory information.

Peer group A group of people of about the same age and interests.

Peripheral Situated on the edge of something.

Phenomenon (plural: phenomena) An observable fact, condition, or event.

Physiological Concerning the way living organisms and their body parts work.

Polygamous Relating to one person with several marriage partners.

Reflex An action performed without conscious thought in response to a stimulus.

Rudiment A basic, primitive form of something.

Schema A model or outline of a theory.

Schizophrenia A long-term mental disorder characterized by abnormalities in the perception or expression of reality.

Sibling A brother or sister.

Synthesize Combine several things into a coherent whole.

Taxonomic Concerned with classification.

Temporal cortex Part of the cerebral cortex; it plays an important part in hearing, speech, vision, and long-term memory.

Teratogens Environmental factors that can affect the development of the fetus.

Torso The trunk of the human body.

Ultrasound Sound waves with a frequency above human hearing that are often used in medical imaging.

Variable Something whose value is subject to change.

Vestibular system A series of liquid-filled canals located in the inner ear.

Visual acuity Sharpness or keenness of sight.

Visual cortex The area of the brain concerned with vision.

Further Research

BOOKS

Davis, R. D., and Braun, E. M. *The Gift of Dyslexia: Why Some of the Smartest People Can't Read and How They Can Learn*. New York: Perigee, 2010.

Eliot, L. *What's Going on in There? How the Brain and Mind Develop in the First Five Years of Life*. New York: Bantam Books, 2000.

Goswami, U. *Cognition in Children*. London, UK: Psychology Press, 1998.

Grandin, T. *Thinking in Pictures: My Life with Autism*. New York: Vintage Books, 2010.

Halford, G. S. *Children's Understanding: The Development of Mental Models*. Hillsdale, NJ: Lawrence Erlbaum Associates, 1993.

Holmes, J. *John Bowlby and Attachment Theory*. New York: Routledge, 1993.

Johnson, M. J. *Developmental Cognitive Neuroscience*. Cambridge, MA: Blackwell, 2005.

Jusczyk, P. W. *The Discovery of Spoken Language*. Cambridge, MA: MIT Press, 2000.

Karen, R. *Becoming Attached: First Relationships and How They Shape Our Capacity to Love*. New York: Oxford University Press, 1998.

Levelt, W. J. M. *Speaking: From Intention to Articulation*. Cambridge, MA: MIT Press, 1993.

McCabe, D. *To Teach a Dyslexic*. Clio, MI: AVKO Educational Research, 1997.

Obler, L. K. and Gjerlow, K. *Language and the Brain*. New York: Cambridge University Press, 1999.

Pinker, S. *The Language Instinct*. New York: HarperPerennial, 2007.

Rutter, M. *Genes and Behavior: Nature-Nurture Interplay Explained*. Wiley-Blackwell, 2006.

Savage-Rumbaugh, S., Shanker, S. G., and Taylor, T. J. *Apes, Language, and the Human Mind*. New York: Oxford University Press, 2001.

Siegler, R. S. and Alibali, Martha W. *Children's Thinking (4th edition)*. Englewood Cliffs, NJ: Prentice Hall, 2004.

Singer, D. G. and Singer, J. L. (eds.). *Handbook of Children and the Media*. Thousand Oaks, CA: Sage Publications, 2001.

Vygotsky, L. S. *Mind in Society: The Development of Higher Psychological Processes*. Cambridge, MA: Harvard University Press, 1978.

Werner, E. E. and Smith, R. S. *Overcoming the Odds: High-Risk Children from Birth to Adulthood*. Ithaca, NY: Cornell University Press, 1992.

INTERNET RESOURCES

Amazing Optical Illusions. See your favorite optical illusions at this fun site.
www.optillusions.com

American Psychological Association. Here you can follow the development of new ethical guidelines for pscychologists, and find a wealth of other information.
www.apa.org

Association for Behavioral and Cognitive Therapies. An interdisciplinary organization concerned with the application of behavioral and cognitive sciences to the understanding of human behavior.
www.abct.org

Exploratorium. Click on "seeing" or "hearing" to check out visual and auditory illusions and other secrets of the mind.
www.exploratorium.edu/exhibits/nf_exhibits.html

Great Ideas in Personality. This website looks at scientific research programs in personality psychology. Pages on attachment theory, basic emotions, behavior genetics, behaviorism, cognitive social theories, and more give concise definitions of terms as well as links to further research on the web.
www.personalityresearch.org

Kidspsych. American Psychological Association's children's site, with games and exercises for kids. Also useful for students of developmental psychology.
www.kidspsych.org/index1.html

Neuroscience for Kids. A useful website for students and teachers who want to learn about the nervous system. Enjoy activities and experiments on your way to learning all about the brain and spinal cord.
faculty.washington.edu/chudler/neurok.html

Neuroscience Tutorial. The Washington University School of Medicine's online tutorial offers an illustrated guide to the basics of clinical neuroscience, with useful artworks and user-friendly text.
thalamus.wustl.edu/course

Personality Theories. An electronic textbook covering personality theories for undergraduate and graduate courses.
www.webspace.ship.edu/cgboer/perscontents.html

Seeing, Hearing, and Smelling the World. A downloadable illustrated book dealing with perception from the Howard Hughes Medical Institute.
www.hhmi.org/senses/

Social Psychology Network. One of the largest social psychology databases on the Internet. Within these pages you will find more than 5,000 links to psychology-related resources and research groups, and there is also a useful section on general psychology.
www.socialpsychology.org

Index